□□□

The Ancient Theatre

ERIKA SIMON

The
Ancient Theatre

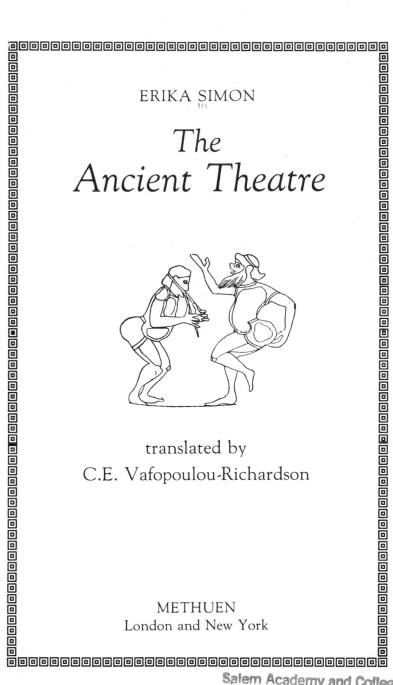

translated by

C.E. Vafopoulou-Richardson

METHUEN
London and New York

First published as *Das Antike Theater*
by Ploetz GmB H und Co., West Germany
© 1972 Ploetz GmB H und Co.

English translation of the revised version
published in Germany in 1981
first published in 1982
by Methuen & Co. Ltd
11 New Fetter Lane, London EC4P 4EE

Published in the USA
by Methuen & Co. Ltd
in association with Methuen, Inc.
733 Third Avenue, New York, NY 10017

© 1982 Methuen & Co. Ltd

Typeset in Hong Kong by Graphicraft Typesetters
Printed in Great Britain by
J.W. Arrowsmith Ltd, Bristol

British Library Cataloguing in Publication Data
Simon, Erika
The ancient theatre.
1. Theater—Greece   2. Theather—Rome
I. Title   II. Das antike Theater, *English*
792'.0938   PA3201

ISBN 0-416-32520-3
ISBN 0-416-32530-0 Pbk

Contents

List of plates

1 Flute player and maenad from a tragic chorus.
2 Tragic chorus invoking a ghost by its grave.
3 Votive relief from Piraeus showing three actors, probably from Euripides' *Bacchae*, in the presence of Dionysus.
4 1 Mask of a young tragic heroine or chorus girl.
   2 Mask of a young tragic chorus girl.
   3 Actor carrying mask of tragic king, probably that of Tereus, from Sophocles' tragedy of that name.
5 Actor and mask of a royal character from tragedy.
6 1 Actors rehearsing: a maenad and young Dionysus.
   2 A comic chorus: men dressed in women's clothes and shoes.
7 1 & 2 Chorus from Aeschylus' satyr play *The Sphinx*.
8 1 & 2 Banqueting Dionysus and *silenos* as *kitharodes*; the satyr Mimus as flute player.
9 Actors and chorus of a satyr play, perhaps Demetrios' *Omphale*.
10 Backdrop (*skenographia*) for a tragedy.
11 1 Backdrop (*skenographia*) for a satyr play, possibly Aeschylus' *Amymone*.
   2 Backdrop (*skenographia*) for New Comedy.
12 1 Mask of an old woman from New Comedy.
   2 Mask of a *hetaira* from New Comedy.
13 Scene from the beginning of Menander's *Synaristosai*.
14 *Phylax* farce.
15 'Telephus travestitus'.
16 Tragic actor of the Roman Imperial period.

Preface

Erika Simon's *Das Antike Theater* first appeared in 1972 and has been extensively used since by both archaeologists and philologists. In recent years the interest and the potential popularity of the subject made her realize the need for a revised version. It is this version which I am now offering to the English reader on both sides of the Atlantic, with the hope that it will thus become accessible to an even larger public.

In its concise and clear form the book is an excellent introduction to the history of the Greek theatre. Its brief and well-documented sections offer an invaluable starting point from which both the general reader and the specialist can go on to a more detailed study of this subject.

The idea for a translation was first conceived when I encountered the problem that so many of my students to whom I recommended the book were unable to read it in the original language. I am in debt to all of them for encouraging me to embark on this task. I am also grateful to my former tutor, John Barron, who first suggested the possibility of having it published, to Erika Simon, who responded to this venture with kindness and enthusiasm, and also to Oliver Taplin for his assistance in the publication of the work.

Many have guided me along the sensitive path of translation, and they should find here the expression of my extensive gratitude. But my special thanks go to John Kerrigan, John Boardman and my husband, all of whom read the manuscript in all its phases and helped to improve its clarity.

Ancient Greek theatre

For the understanding of drama, more than any other branch of
ancient Greek literature, we are dependent on archaeological sources,
because as an art form ancient Greek drama involved not only the
words and music of the poet, but also the costume of the actors and
the arrangement of the theatre. It was, one might say, a multi-
dimensional work of art (*Gesamtkunstwerk*).

It is clear from the ancient biographies of Aeschylus, Sophocles and
Euripides just how big a part was played by non-literary factors in the
original performances in the theatre of Dionysus at Athens. Innovations in the use of actors, masks, theatrical machines or scenery are
ascribed to each of these dramatists; and as such innovations are part
of the history of figurative art rather than of the spoken word they are
best reconstructed by archaeological methods.

However, we tend to be sceptical nowadays of historical reconstructions, and our producers prefer to stage tragedies (whether of
Aeschylus Shakespeare or Schiller) either in an abstract form which
concentrates purely on the words, or otherwise in the style of their
own period. Something similar was already the case with the revival of
classical plays in antiquity. There is no fundamental objection to such
modernization, for the production of plays which are hundreds or
even thousands of years old naturally involves a degree of com-
promise. On the other hand, it is certain that contemporary adapta-
tions of ancient tragedies and comedies usually last for only one
generation on the stage, whereas ancient originals (even in feeble
translations and productions) are imperishable. From this one can
conclude that, however much these poetic works may be rooted in a
certain period, they possess a timeless quality and still speak to men
and women of the present day. Archaeological material can also give
an ancient play life as a comprehensive work of art.

Let us first examine the appearance of the theatre of Dionysus on
the south slope of the Athenian Acropolis, for it was the prototype of
all later Greek theatres. It was for this setting that Aeschylus,
Sophocles and Euripides created their tragedies.[1]

The most important observation is that, in contrast to our play-houses, the building had no roof. This should not be ascribed to the theatre's fragmentary preservation, but is a peculiarity due to its original character and nature. It was open and public, a concern for all the Athenian people, who provided actors and choruses and selected the victor from the three dramatists who competed for the prize at annual performances. Since plays were staged in the open air, the chorus in, for example, the opening song of Sophocles' *Antigone* actually greets the first rays of the sun. The dramatic performances began in the morning of the first day and continued for three consecutive days, during which the three tetralogies by the dramatists who had been chosen by the Proagon[2] were performed. The three most important elements in the Greek theatre are the *orchestra*, the *theatron* and the *skene*. These terms are still used today, but with different meanings. The characteristic form of the three parts of the theatre is best explained by a ground plan. Since the theatre of Dionysus suffered structural alterations down to late antiquity, and these are the subject of scholarly debate, other theatre plans are more suitable for illustration. A particularly clear plan is that of the theatre of

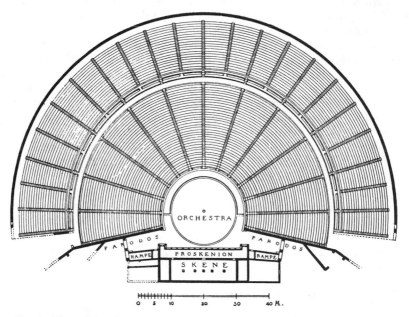

Fig. 1 Plan of the theatre at Epidaurus. From Dorpfeld-Reisch (see note 1), 122, fig. 50.

Epidaurus (built in the late fourth century BC), whose harmony and beauty Pausanias praises above all other ancient theatrical constructions in his *Description of Greece* (II, 27,5).[3]

The orchestra

In the Greek theatre plays were not produced on a box-shaped, enclosed stage raised over the spectators' rows of seats, but on a wide circle of flat ground, the *orchestra*. This means, literally, 'dancing place' (ὀρχεῖσθαι = to dance). The circular form of the *orchestra* leads one to conclude that, originally, ring dances were performed there. Dances of this kind are very old and Homer, for example, compared the movement of dancers with the turning of a potter's wheel (*Il.* 18.599ff.). Many Greek villages today still have a circular place, the threshing floor (ἡ ἅλως; in modern Greek τὸ ἁλώνι), where corn is threshed, and which at festivals is used as a dancing floor.

Drama developed from peasant dances, for it was produced in honour of a god—Dionysus—who was worshipped especially by the peasants. His cult acquired great importance in Greece in the Archaic period, when the city-states were governed by sole rulers, the so-called tyrants, who encouraged the cult of Dionysus for the benefit of the peasant population on whose support their rule relied. So the festival of the 'Great Dionysia', which took place in Athens in spring, and at which dramatic performances were given, was reorganized by the tyrant Pisistratus. In this period we find the first recorded performance of Thespis, who won the Athenian competition for tragedies in 534 BC.[4]

According to Aristotle (cf. *Poetics* 1449a), tragedy developed from the leading singers of the dithyramb, which is described by ancient authors as a κύκλιος χορός (= 'circular dance'), whereas the dances in tragedy, satyr plays and comedy are described as 'rectangular', because the dramatic choruses moved in straight lines.[5] The transition from circular to linear dancing accordingly belongs to the history of the development of drama, which reached its classic form in the fifth century BC. The circular dance of the dithyramb did not, however, die out. In the *orchestra* of the theatre of Dionysus dithyrambs as well as tragedies were regularly performed for competition at the 'Great Dionysia'.[6] The *orchestra's* circular form thus reflects choral dancing of the period before the introduction of drama. It is significant that the Greeks should have retained the traditional circular dancing place, despite the unprecedented linear development of their drama. It was the oldest part, and it dictated the overall plan of the Greek theatre down to late antiquity.

In his excavations of the interior of the theatre of Dionysus in Athens, W. Dörpfeld uncovered a circle approximately 20 m. in diameter, which he interpreted as the sixth-century *orchestra*.[7] In its centre must have stood an altar, which the ancient sources refer to as *thymele*.[8] The *orchestra* was immediately next to the small, older temple of Dionysus, whose foundations have been found. Dionysus there bore the epithet of Eleuthereus, because his cult was introduced to Athens from Eleutherai, on the boundary between Attica and Boeotia. Boeotia paid special honour to Dionysus: the god was supposed to have been born in Thebes. In memory of his Boeotian origin the cult statue of Eleuthereus (a pillar-shaped idol of Dionysus)[9] was each year solemnly transported from the north to Athens as a prelude to the 'Great Dionysia', and erected in the sacred precinct at the foot of the Acropolis. Dithyrambs and dramas were performed in front of this cult statue, originally purely as acts of worship rather than as performances directed at spectators.

The theatron

The name with which we today designate the theatre as a whole originally only referred to the area occupied by the spectators. It can be derived from $\vartheta\epsilon\tilde{\alpha}\sigma\vartheta\alpha\iota$, 'to look at'. Corresponding to the circular form of the orchestra, this part was also circular, or rather bowl-shaped, for it rested on a natural slope. In Athens this was the south slope of the Acropolis. The hill may be steeper, as at Pergamum, or more gentle, as at Epidaurus (where it is beautifully embedded in the landscape). But the existence of a hill was indispensable for the Greek theatre's design. The *theatron* surrounded approximately two-thirds of the *orchestra*.

There are various reasons why the originally independent cult-dances in honour of Dionysus gradually acquired more and more spectators. In the first place the Dionysia was a popular festival, when work ceased and leisure was available for spectacles — and how ready the Greeks were to be spectators, particularly the Athenians of the Archaic period. This was the period when the spectator — with all his responses to any event — began to appear in pictorial art. Spectators frame athletic competitions, mythical adventures and even scenes on the battle-field in vase paintings of the period. A fragment by the vase painter Sophilos (c. 570 BC) shows a grandstand from which Achilles and the Achaeans watch the games in honour of his dead friend Patroclus. It is probably a wooden stand, similar to those ($\H{\iota}\varkappa\varrho\iota\alpha$) still used in the Athenian theatres of the fifth century BC.[10]

Apart from the god Dionysus-Eleuthereus, the principal spectator was his priest, who had his seat in the middle of the front row of the *theatron*. Beside him sat other priests and high officials in seats of honour (the *prohedria*). Together with the people they decided to which of the competing poets the prize of victory was to be awarded. This element of contest (ἀγών), so characteristic of the Greeks, was a further reason for the constant increase in the number of spectators in the theatre. The splendidly decorated priest's throne in the theatre of Dionysus, for example, shows cocks, as a symbol of the contest, being urged to fight by winged boys. It has been shown that this throne belongs to the fourth century BC, the period of the first stone construction of the theatre of Dionysus.[11]

At the time of the three great tragedians all inner parts of the theatre were built of perishable material. Only the outer, surrounding wall of the *theatron* was of stone, as was usually the case with the walls of sacred precincts. In fact the theatre belonged to the sanctuary of Dionysus-Eleuthereus. Not until the period of Alexander the Great, under the Attic statesman Lycurgus, was the theatre of Dionysus rebuilt in stone. Typical of the engineering skill of that period was the beautiful and well-designed partition of the *theatron*, which is arranged in tiers of seats ascending the slope and running in concentric arcs. Two broad horizontal passages or gangways (διαζώματα) divide the rows of seats into three bands, to ease the entrance and exit of the crowds of spectators. For the same reason radial staircases are placed at intervals, separating the *theatron* vertically into wedge-shaped sections (κερκίδες). The Lycurgan theatre of Dionysus could hold 14,000 to 17,000 spectators.[12] In today's performances at the theatre of Epidaurus (fig. 1) one can still see how, thanks to its well-planned design, many thousands of spectators can both fill and leave the theatre in a relatively short time.

The skene

That segment of the *orchestra* not surrounded by the rows of seats of the *theatron* was closed by the *skene*: between, on either side, lay the *parodos* (fig. 1), through which the chorus entered (their entry song is also called *parodos*). Σκηνή is sometimes translated as 'tent' or 'hut', which is misleading, and one must imagine a wooden construction with a flat roof.[13] Its existence is explained by the development of the drama, which was obviously closely linked to the development of theatre design. In the Archaic period there was only one actor, who 'answered' or 'reported to' (ὑποκριτης) the chorus. The original importance of the chorus is shown by the fact that this reporting is directed entirely at them. Aeschylus reduced the prominence of the chorus and introduced a second actor, and Sophocles a third. Changes of costume for the different roles which the actor assumed (as the plays frequently involved more than two or three characters) took place in the σκηνή, the wooden structure on the border of the *orchestra*, during interludes when the chorus sang. Originally it was certainly small, and was only later enlarged and extended in accordance with the more complicated character of the plays. It is assumed that the technical equipment of the stage, as well as masks and other theatrical props, was also kept in it, and some of the wooden stands for the spectators and the priests' seats could also have been stored there when not needed. The lengthy wooden structure served at the same time as the back wall of the stage, and thus the name *skene* (Latin *scaenae frons*) was preserved; we still speak of theatrical scenes and scenery.

In the course of time the third part of the Greek theatre, the *skene*, underwent more extensive alterations than the other two parts. In the theatre of Dionysus the stone foundations for the *skene* (which was itself still made of wood) date from the pre-Lycurgan phase of the fourth century BC.[14] How these foundations are to be interpreted is not yet entirely clear, and on the basis of their form it is debatable whether this late classical *skene* also had projecting wings (*paraskenia*) on either side. The recent excavations in the theatre of Dionysus, which have not yet been published, may possibly give a more definite picture.[15]

Recent literary research has shown particular interest in the staging of surviving plays, and the archaeological reconstruction of the classical stage has profited from this. Thus it has been shown that from the time of Aeschylus dramatists must have used the *ekkyklema*, a wheeled platform, with the help of which events 'behind the scenes' were brought before the eyes of the spectators.[16] In addition Aeschylus already appears to have used a crane-like flying machine,[17] which was later used especially by Euripides, and which Aristophanes ridiculed in his comedies. However, it appears that Old Comedy no less than tragedy needed a variety of gadgets on the stage.

Hans-Joachim Newiger has recently shown that for the 421 BC production of Aristophanes' *Peace* three doors in the *skene* must be assumed.[18] We will come to the problem of the number of doors in tragic performances when we discuss stage painting. It should be said in advance that this problem must be considered not only from the viewpoint of the strict interpretation of the text, but also from that of aesthetics, since the lengthy stage-building, which often had to represent a king's palace, would have been broken up and divided into parts by the addition of two doors to the right and left of the main central door. The doors could be present without being used, however, for the door was a favourite decorative motif in ancient art.[19]

A high stage, which we are used to, did not exist at the time of the three great tragedians, but there were probably some broad steps leading from the level of the *skene* to the *orchestra*;[20] and in Aeschylus' plays actors sometimes appeared on the flat roof of the wooden stage, like the watchman posted by Clytemnestra at the beginning of the *Oresteia*. This level also represented the *theologeion* from which the gods intervene in the action in Euripides' plays. In general the spectator saw the action in the classical period 'in the round', since the chorus danced and sang in the *orchestra*, and the actors of individual roles made their way into it.

In the Hellenistic period the *orchestra* gradually lost its role as an acting place, for in the later plays the chorus takes no part in the action, as one can infer from the recently discovered texts of Menander. Plays now took place on a raised stage ($\pi\rho o\sigma\kappa\eta\nu\iota o\nu$), which was projected in front of the 'first floor' of the stage-building: the spectators saw the action 'in relief'. A layout of this Hellenistic form can be seen in the well-preserved small theatre at Oropos in Attica.[21] In addition to performances of New Comedy many classical tragedies were revived, so the Hellenistic *skene* must have been very versatile.

The Romans took over the Hellenistic high stage and altered it, together with the whole building, in a characteristic way.[22] The theatre in this period was not composed of many loosely united elements, embedded in the natural setting — as, for example, is the theatre at Epidaurus (fig. 1) — but was a unified architectural complex. It no longer rested on the slope of a hill, but stood on level ground. The Roman *theatron* (in Latin, *cavea*), was built over vaulted passages, such as are also found in their elliptically-shaped amphitheatres. The theatre at Orange in Provence, from the early Imperial period, is still, admittedly, built into a hill,[23] but the three-storeyed *scaenae frons*, which is generally well-preserved, is integrated with the *cavea* into one single compact construction, which may have been covered with a big awning.[24] The stage front of Orange only lacks the marble facing. One can see what this may have looked like from the *scaenae frons* of the theatre at Sabratha in Libya, which is built entirely on level ground and has been reconstructed by the Italian excavators.[25] The well-known theatre of Herodes Atticus on the south-west slope of the Athenian Acropolis belongs to the same period, the late second century AD.[26] The lofty *scaenae frons* with its powerful arches makes it a structure conceived very differently from the nearby theatre of Dionysus. The latter's original, circular *orchestra* is reduced to a semicircle in the theatre of Herodes Atticus, as is the case in other theatres of the Imperial period. The chorus sings and dances in it today at the performances of ancient plays which take place throughout the summer. The modern Greek performances have revived this oldest element of ancient drama in a remarkable way. The reason is that modern Greek choruses understand how to pray, dance, entreat and, above all, lament in the ancient manner, as hardly any other modern dramatic chorus can.

The chorus

From the beginning dancing formed one of the most important parts of the cult of Dionysus. The word χορός is applied equally to the dancers and singers and to their performance.[27] From it all three kinds of drama — tragedy, satyr play and comedy — developed. On Attic vases of the Archaic period numerous Dionysiac scenes are preserved, in which the god stands peacefully in the middle, while his retinue dance round him. Normally the vase painters represent the god himself instead of his statue, and instead of the human chorus his mythical retinue in the form of satyrs and maenads. The impersonation was easy, since during the celebrations the dancers in the *orchestra* transformed themselves into these mythical beings by their clothing and masks. Theatre props are also rare in fifth-century Attic vase painting. The painters' imagination was so great that they could translate the action on the stage directly into myth. They portrayed what contemporary spectators saw in the tragedies: the myth itself.

It is rather different with comedy and its predecessors: here Archaic painters already occasionally alluded to the actor's disguise, which formed an important part of the comic effect (cf. fig. 3). The same is true of the members of the satyr play's chorus, whose kilts were sometimes already shown by the painters of the early fifth century BC. Consequently it is more difficult to point to tragic scenes on vase-painting than to scenes from other types of drama. In addition, before the Hellenistic period, illustrations in the strict sense — that is, referring to particular passages in the text — are not found.[28] The first surviving examples are of the New Comedy of Menander (cf. pl. 13). Because of these difficulties, it is understandable that in earlier archaeological works on classical tragedy only Attic vase paintings of the period around 400 BC, and above all Apulian vases of the fourth century BC, were discussed.[29] But in recent times some evidence has emerged which widens our conception of the early dramatic chorus.

A red-figured *crater* (mixing bowl) in the Museum of Antiquities at Basle, dated by its style to about 500-490 BC and made in Athens (pl. 2),[30] shows a chorus of six young men in its main scene with masks on their heads and wearing short, decorated garments. They dance, in pairs and with identical movements, in front of an architectural construction which was previously identified (even by me) as an altar. As it lacks spirals this is impossible. It was Karl Schefold who realised that it must be a tomb, at which the dead man appears, invoked by the chorus.[31] The tragic chorus was probably composed in this period of twelve members (later, at the time of Sophocles and Euripides, there were fifteen). The painter therefore shows half the participants, possibly one wing of them, arranged in ranks.[32] On this vase we have possibly the earliest surviving pictorial evidence of the basic form of tragedy, the dance of the chorus in the *orchestra*. When one considers this picture, the few remains of the Archaic layout which W. Dörpfeld found in the theatre of Dionysus are filled with life. We cannot know the specific pre-Aeschylean drama which inspired the vase scene. The ritual of lamentation for a dead man which, to judge by their gestures, the dancers are performing was certainly even then an essential part of early tragedies. In any case the piece strongly impressed the vase painter, who must have been seated in the audience.

The painter of the vase in the museum in Basle has omitted the musician, to whose melody the chorus danced. He must have been a player of the double αὐλός, an instrument which we usually translate as 'pipe'. It was less like our modern pipes, however, than an oboe. Such an αὐλός-player is represented (pl. 1)[33] on an Attic vase dating from about 470 BC, in Berlin's Charlottenburg Museum, wearing the professional dress of musicians, a long, decorated tunic (*chiton*), with sleeves; the sleeves are here part of the tunic, while those of the actors, as we will see, were stitched on separately. The player wears the φορβεία, the leather mouth-band, which helped him to blow. Before him a maenad dances, clad in a short tunic, holding in her right hand a sword and in her raised left the bleeding leg of a deer. She differs from many maenads on contemporary vase paintings in her unusual hairstyle, which shoots up above her forehead like a little flame and flows in long, stiff strands around her shoulders and neck. As hair in that period was generally rendered more softly and naturally, the vase painter may have intended to show artificial hair, that is, the wig of a mask: since the masks of ancient actors covered not only the face but the whole of the head, hair was sometimes also attached to them (cf. pl.4). It is true that the maenad, like all other roles in the Greek theatre, would have had to be acted by a man, but the vase painters were not so obviously explicit. The scene dates from Aeschylus' period, and gives us a notion of the effect a chorus of maenads had on the spectators in the theatre of that time. Among the recorded titles of Aeschylean plays are both *Bacchae* and *Bassarae*, in both of which the chorus was composed of maenads. In fact, some dramatic choruses as far back as the sixth century must have been composed of maenads.

The tragic costume

In all three types of drama, tragedy, satyr plays and comedy, the actors were heavily disguised, much more than in the modern theatre. This was due not only to the fact that the female roles were played by men, but ultimately had its roots in religion. A complete disguise was the external sign that the actor had given up his own identity in honour of the god, in order to let another being speak and act through him. Dionysus, for whom the dramas were performed, was the god of ecstasy. The word ἔχστασις means 'standing outside oneself'; in other words the renunciation of individuality. An important medium for this in all three types of drama was the mask (τὸ πρόσωπον).

The earliest tragic masks which are preserved in painting are found on the *crater* in Basle (pl. 2). As the chin lines are clearly rendered, they are certainly masks (which would have included the diadem and the hair; for, as we have said, the ancient actor's mask covered the whole head). The mouth is slightly open, and in front of it are written letters (only visible on the vase itself), which refer to the song of the chorus. It is not always understood that ancient theatrical masks were not stiff and immovable but were worn by players who acted, spoke and sang.[34] To judge from the pictorial evidence in the period of the earlier Attic dramatists (pl. 2; 4,1) the mouth-opening of the masks was small, but from the time of the later plays of Euripides onwards it became larger (pl. 3; 4,2). The mask with gaping mouth is first attested from about 300 BC, both for tragic (pl. 5) and for comic characters (pl. 12). It appears that this later shape of mouth was also intended to produce a certain effect of resonance.

The mask of a young tragic heroine or chorus girl of Aeschylus' period is shown on a red-figure jug which was excavated in the Athenian Agora (pl. 4,1).[35] A servant-boy (not visible on our detail) holds the masks from a loop in his lowered hand, while around him actors in women's clothes are preparing themselves for the performance or dress rehearsal. The mask's hair, through which a band runs, is cut short as a sign of mourning. The face, with its regular features, clearly arched brows and straight nose, recalls sculptured heads of about 460 BC, the height of the so-called Severe style. A particularly good comparison is with the head of the bride who is being carried off by a centaur on the west pediment of the temple of Zeus at Olympia.[36] From comparisons of this kind one can conclude that during the period of the three great dramatists the masks reflected the general artistic development of their time, and that their style did not differ from that of contemporary sculpture. Since the pictorial artists of the classical period displayed expressions of sorrow, fear or exertion only in a very restrained way on the faces of their figures, this must also have been the case with tragic masks. Unfortunately no original example is preserved, since the theatrical masks were made from light, perishable materials (wood, plaster, wool, linen). But their imitations on vase paintings speak clearly to us.

In contrast to the mask from the Agora, whose effect is so calm (pl. 4,1), the mask of a young tragic-chorus singer on a vase painting of about 400 BC is shown with wild, curly hair and a look of pathos (pl. 4,2).[37] The wider opening of the mouth has already been discussed. These features are no longer explicable in terms of the development of contemporary large-scale sculpture. Towards the end of the fifth century a separate development of theatrical masks began, which continued right into the Roman period. Masks of this new design already appear to have been worn in the later dramas of Euripides. As evidence for this one can cite the actors' relief from Piraeus (pl. 3).[38] The three actors standing in front of the reclining Dionysus have been convincingly connected with the *Bacchae* of Euripides. The maenad sitting on the god's couch probably personifies the chorus of Bacchants from that tragedy, which was first performed in Athens in 406 BC, shortly after the death of the playwright. The actor standing at the left side with the *tympanon* (tambourine) played Agave's role. He had put on his mask, which unfortunately is not preserved. The two others carry their masks in their hands. Despite the weathering of the marble's surface we can discern that the mouth-opening of the mask corresponds with that of the mask represented on pl. 4,2. While the early masks were similar to contemporary sculptures, now the hair, brows, eyes and mouth were fashioned in a specifically stylized and 'mask-like' way.

With this background we are able to understand how the actor's real face and his mask, which he removed for the applause, could be so different in features as those on the famous 'Player' fragment in Würzburg (pl. 4,3).[39] The face of the performer, with the broad nose, curled lips, stubbly beard, and scanty, greying hair, forms the most extreme contrast with the noble blond king's mask in his right hand. The picture was painted around 340 BC in Tarentum, and the actor probably played the Thracian king Tereus in the Sophoclean tragedy of that name, of which only fragments have survived.

About a generation later the same scene was painted again and we have a good copy preserved on stucco from Herculaneum, the city which was destroyed by Vesuvius (pl. 5).[40] Once more a successful

11

actor is depicted after the performance. The sceptre, sword and purple mantle which are assigned to him point to a royal role. The mask which he wore and at which he looks is set up on the right as a votive offering by the kneeling maiden, possibly the personification of the *skene*. On the mask with its darkly shadowed eyes the high bow-shaped addition to the hair above the forehead is a new element. This is the ὄγκος, which appeared on tragic masks towards 300 BC, and which continued to define their appearance in the Roman Imperial period (pl. 16).[41] With this addition the mask presented a 'façade' in its frontal view. It fitted well with the high stage which was introduced in the same period. While the actors had previously performed in the orchestra, where one could see them from all sides, now, owing to the new form of the stage, they could only be seen from certain angles. The mask with the ὄγκος appears to have produced its best effect in a three-quarter view, for it is frequently represented thus in pictorial art (pl. 5). But however much masks of this form may still influence the modern conception of the ancient tragic stage, they were not part of the theatre of the three great dramatists.

Besides the mask, the tragic actor's equipment also included a costume with long sleeves and a special type of boot, the *kothornos*. The author of the late *Life of Aeschylus* ascribes the introduction of both to this poet, and we should probably understand this to mean that such a costume was usual in the period of Aeschylus: its origin is still disputed today by scholars.[42] The dress of the Eleusinian priests, or that of the Persian kings, have been considered as models. Both views can be refuted. Not only the actors of the principal roles but also those of the secondary ones and the chorus were dressed with *kothornoi* and sleeves, and certainly no Persian royal splendour would have been displayed in these cases. Moreover, the most important part of Persian dress, the *tiara* on the head, would have been missing. The priests of Eleusis did not wear the soft, broad boots of the actor, but close-fitting, laced boots with flaps — that is to say, typical riding boots — since, according to legend, their ancestor Eumolpus had come from Thrace, a land of horsemen.[43] Margarete Bieber, who contributed much to research on the ancient theatre, believed that the actors adopted their dress from Dionysus himself, the god of the theatre. But this cannot be right either, for the numerous representations of Dionysus in sixth- and fifth-century vase painting usually show him in Ionic dress, that is in *chiton* and *himation*, but not with the actor's *kothornoi*.[44] He occasionally wears these later — as on a red-figure Calyx *crater* in Boston[45] painted about 380 BC (pl. 6) — but here they are adopted from the actors. Dionysus is thereby characterized as god of the theatre.

The archaeological evidence therefore forbids the derivation of tragic costume from a particular model. It was rather a new creation, in which the early dramatists before Aeschylus shared, a new creation in the sense that various parts of the costume which were already in use were combined to make a new ensemble. The impetus came from the demand which the Dionysiac cult made on the actor to give up his own identity and to allow someone else to speak and act through him. In addition to this basic religious demand, aesthetic and practical aspects also had their effect on the development of the drama.

In the view of the Greeks, a mask which only covered the head was not sufficient to eliminate the personality of the actor. For them, as we know from their art, the body of a man was no less individual than the head. Thus, with the portrait (the creation of the realistic portrait coincides with the period of Aeschylus),[46] they did not confine themselves to the head, but represented the whole body, in the 'portrait statue'. Accordingly, the long sleeves of the actor served primarily for disguise, like the mask. One must also bear in mind that there were no actresses; the many female roles were played by male actors. Women's skin tended to be painted lighter than that of men in Greek pictorial art.[47] Thus it is possible that the long white sleeves in many female roles might simply indicate the skin, particularly as they were not cut with the overgarment, but were part of an undergarment. In the Life of Aeschylus sleeves (χειρῖδες) are explicitly mentioned as a particular part of the actor's costume. On the vase from Naples (pl. 9) of about 400 BC, depicting a satyr play (see p. 17), all sleeves are in fact shown with multicoloured ornament, but the play represented here was set in a Lydian palace in Asia Minor, and the dress was suited to that ambience. The Lydians were known for their multicoloured, richly-decorated clothes. Thus on this same vase the boots of both actors who stand near the couch of Dionysus are decorated with patterns, while otherwise they are plain.

The definition of the kothornos in ancient dictionaries, and also in archaeological discussions of the Greek theatre, leaves something to be desired.[48] The word κόθορνος can indeed signify different kinds of boot, but in the field of dramatic costume only a particular type, related neither to the elegantly laced travelling boots of the messenger nor to the tightly-fitting riding boots of the Thracians (which are laced and equipped with flaps). Such boots were indeed occasionally used on stage, but only when the role required it, as in the scene with the Thracians in Aeschylus' Lycurgus trilogy or in Sophocles' Tereus. Probably the kothornoi in their original form were used and camouflaged in accordance with the role, as shown on the satyr play vase where they have become a fine Lydian type of boot (pl. 9). The original *kothornoi* were soft and wide, with toes fashioned in a beak-shaped tip. At the time of the three great dramatists the soles were low, and not raised as many ancient dictionaries describe. The idea of raised soles derives from the later author of the *Life of Aeschylus*, who ascribed to this poet the introduction of the high *kothornoi*, but is clearly contra-dicted by the archaeological evidence which always shows the *kothornoi* in the classical period as low. The example reproduced here (pl. 6,1) shows two actors rehearsing.[49] One of them wears a maenad's mask over his head, and also the deer skin, the maenad's *nebris*, and performs an ecstatic dance. The actor facing him holds a mask in his hand, perhaps (as Giuliana Riccioni suggests) that of the young Dionysus. His flat pointed shoes are drawn frontally, while those of his companion are shown in profile. Aeschylus' biographer was describing the stilt-like *kothornoi* of the Roman Imperial period (pl. 16), which in recent literature have become the symbol of the tragic style. The raising of the soles, which began no earlier than the Hellenistic period, is comparable with the heightening of the tragic mask by the ὄγκος. Both these additions to the original classical dress had the purpose of making the actor seem taller. The smallness of the performers in relation to their surroundings is a perennial problem of all open-air theatres, but in the period of the three great dramatists an attempt was made to solve this problem in another way (see p. 27).

Red-figure vase representations at the time of Aeschylus give us a sure indication of the source of the high, broad, pointed shoes of the actors: the ladies' quarters.[50] At that time courtesans, particularly, used these comfortable, soft house shoes, which they placed under the couch at the symposium. In the subsequent cheerful revellers' proces-sion it often happened that a banqueter put on the shoes of his girl-friend, especially as they were easily put on even in a drunken state since there was no distinction between right and left. However, when a man wore pointed shoes the Greeks generally took this as a sign of effeminacy.[51] Thus the six bearded chorus singers on a recently discovered cup by the Sabouroff painter (pl. 6,2) are shown with long tunics, pointed shoes, and with feminine movements.[52] They must be the chorus of a comedy, the type of drama which did not use *kothornoi*, but for which men in women's roles were characteristic. One could imagine that the chorus from *The Effeminates* (*Malthakoi*) of the comic playwright Cratinus were portrayed in a similar way. In my opinion the use of *kothornoi* on the stage is due to the way they thoroughly disguise the legs and feet; for it is well known from many works of art, and particularly from late Archaic marble sculptures, that Greek artists were able to represent men's feet in an individual manner. We have seen already that the actor's costume was designed to limit individual features; but possibly still more important than the disguise, the way of walking, an unmistakable sign of individuality also visible from a distance, was standardized by the wearing of the high, broad, pointed shoes. Actors and members of the chorus were thus restricted to a particular form of movement, a stylized gait, suited to the rhythm of the tragic verse.[53]

Tragedy and satyr play

Aristotle, in whose *Poetics* we have the most important ancient sketch of the origin and development of drama, says that tragedy 'was late in becoming serious' (from the context this must mean not long before Aeschylus). Before it suffered this change, it was 'satyric'.[54] The interpretation of this passage is disputed. Aristotle cannot mean that tragedy developed out of the satyr play as we know it, since he himself writes that it originated from the 'leaders of the dithyramb'. In addition we know from other sources that the satyr play was a relatively late creation. Pratinas of Phlius, who competed with the young Aeschylus for the prize, is traditionally known as the 'inventor' of the satyr play. In its structure it was modelled on Archaic tragedy, and not tragedy on it. Certainly the satyr play had a forerunner, namely 'satyrs speaking in verse'. These are supposed to have been introduced by Arion of Lesbos, who was active around 600 BC at the palace of the tyrant of Corinth. The same Arion, according to our sources, also performed the first 'tragic drama', and was the first to give the title 'dithyramb' to a composition. In literary as in archaeological scholarship these pieces of information used to be combined with the above-mentioned passage by Aristotle as follows: the original tragedy of Arion was composed of a satyr chorus, who sang a dithyramb. However Harald Patzer has convincingly removed the 'satyric dithyramb' from the history of Greek literature.[55] He showed that we must distinguish the three separate inventions of Arion. Apart from his modernization of the dithyramb, this poet was reputed to be the creator of the original form of tragedy as well as that of the satyr play, two forms which most probably were composed only of a chorus, without individual actors. That such choruses could also be dramatized in such a way that individual parts sang in competition with each other we know from early choral poetry, for example that of Alcman; in classical tragedy, however, the chorus usually constituted a unity, in contrast to the actors, who performed in alternation with each other.

In the form in which Arion conceived them, tragic and satyric choruses must have continued side by side for about two generations.

15

Unfortunately, for this period (the first half of the sixth century BC) we lack both archaeological and literary evidence. Frank Brommer and Ernst Buschor tried to bridge these gaps with iconographical material, by relating the so-called 'padded dancers', which are particularly frequent on Corinthian vases of this period (fig. 5), to the poetry of Arion, which originated in Corinth.[56] These fat dancers were supposed to be the early satyrs, who sang the dithyramb. Patzer also follows this hypothesis, despite the fact that his theory has destroyed its foundation, by getting rid of the satyric dithyramb. As will be shown in the chapter on comedy the 'padded dancers' are not the ancestors of the satyr play and of tragedy, but clearly of Old Comedy. They are shown as grotesque but purely human forms, whereas the satyrs or silenoi (both names were employed for similar creatures) are hybrid beings with horses' tails and ears. They also sometimes have horses' legs, as on the crater in Florence painted by Cleitias about 570 BC, on which silenoi are attested for the first time by an inscription.[57]

What, then, did Aristotle mean by the statement cited above, that tragedy had developed (after many changes) 'from the satyric' ($\dot{\epsilon}\varkappa$ $\sigma\alpha\tau\upsilon\varrho\iota\varkappa o\tilde{\upsilon}$) into its serious, dignified form? The word $\sigma\alpha\tau\upsilon\varrho\iota\varkappa \acute{o}\nu$, which from a purely linguistic point of view cannot mean the satyr play or the satyr chorus, here indicates the opposite of $\sigma\epsilon\mu\nu \acute{o}\nu$ ('dignified'): Aristotle speaks of making tragedy dignified ($\dot{\alpha}\pi o\sigma\epsilon\mu\nu \acute{\upsilon}\nu\epsilon\sigma\vartheta\alpha\iota$). A definition of 'serious and dignified' is probably imperfect, particularly when we recall that the Erinyes, which Aeschylus brought on to the stage in the last part of the Oresteia, had the cult name Semnai ('awe-inspiring') at Athens. The contrasting word $\sigma\alpha\tau\upsilon\varrho\iota\varkappa \acute{o}\nu$ would be correspondingly difficult to interpret, if the ancient introduction to Euripides' Alcestis did not come to our aid. We know that this piece was performed as the fourth in a tetralogy, that is, instead of a satyr play.[58] However, it is said in the Hypothesis that this drama is $\sigma\alpha\tau\upsilon\varrho\iota\varkappa \acute{\omega}\tau\epsilon\varrho o\nu$, which alludes to the change for the better or happy ending in the Alcestis, which begins tragically but (with the help of Heracles, who here excels himself) ends happily without a catastrophe. Moreover, Euripides' Cyclops, the only complete extant ancient satyr play, ends with the successful attempt upon Polyphemus and the lucky escape of Odysseus and naturally also of the satyrs (although the protagonist does indeed kill two companions of Odysseus: 397ff.). We ought not, then, to make use of the passage of Aristotle to allow satyrs (or indeed padded dancers) to appear in the early form of tragedy. Aristotle wanted rather to say that early tragedy could include happy elements (which later were characteristic of the satyr play), and that the catastrophe, in the sense of the classical 'tragedy', was still missing from it.

From the suggestions made so far it should be clear that tragedy and satyr play were already, in their early phases with Arion, different forms of poetry, but that they were more closely related to each other than either type of drama was to comedy. Comedy had its own poets, while the satyr play was composed by the same poets as tragedy, since it was not independent, but was staged in succession to a tragic trilogy.[59]

Attic vase paintings which refer to satyr plays are found from about 520 BC onwards. Because of the presence of the satyrs they are somewhat easier to detect than vase paintings with tragic stage themes. Frank Brommer has collected a considerable amount of material,[60] and important contributions have since been added, such as the fragment of a calyx *crater* in Würzburg (pl. 8 and fig. 2) and the hydria of the Japanese collector Takuhiko Fujita (pl. 7) which shows Aeschylus' satyr play *The Sphinx*,[61] soon after its production (467 BC). Here five white-haired *silenoi* are shown with the trappings of high office in front of the sphinx who is uttering her riddle. The satyr play vase in Naples, on the other hand, shows a whole chorus (pl. 9).[62] It is assumed that this unusual vase painting reproduces a panel picture which the successful flute player Pronomos dedicated as a thank-offering in the sanctuary of Dionysus (his name and many other names are legible only on the original or in the reproduction in the Furtwängler-Reichhold). Pronomos sits in the middle of the lower row of figures and plays his double pipes. He was a musician of the early fourth century, also known from other sources, who 'through his mime and the movement of his whole body charmed the spectators in the theatre' (Paus. 9.12,6). Between him and the poet Demetrius, who is seated on his left holding a book roll, a satyr dances the *sikinnis*, a wild dance particularly loved by satyrs. In this way the ancient spectator of the picture could virtually hear the music which Pronomos plays. All the other members of the satyr chorus, which appears to be portrayed complete, have removed their masks.[63] To celebrate the success of their piper they remain in the holy precinct of Dionysus, who rests on a couch with his beloved Ariadne in the upper row of figures. Apart from the mask with beard and animal ears, the satyrs' dress consists of shorts, to which are fixed a horse's tail and an erect phallus. Whether the satyr chorus also wore a form of 'tights' as 'stageflesh', cannot be deduced either from this vase painting or from other sources. Possibly the masks and the shorts with their accessories were sufficient disguise for the individuality of these very young members of the chorus. As they had to perform lively dances (for the satyr play often resembled a ballet) the tragic *kothornos* would have been quite unsuitable.

17

The Naples vase painting also gives us important information about the three individual actors in the satyr play. On the right stands the old Papposilenus, who appeared in many satyr plays from the time of Aeschylus. He wears a woollen suit entirely covered with white matted hair, ($\mu\alpha\lambda\lambda\omega\tau\grave{o}\varsigma\ \chi\iota\tau\acute{\omega}\nu$), and holds a white-haired long-bearded mask, in whose mouth-opening only a few teeth are to be seen. The Papposilenus is indeed the 'father' of the satyrs, but it is clear from Euripides' *Cyclops* and from fragments of satyr plays that he was no member of the chorus, but one of the three main actors.[64] Apart from him two more actors stand by the couch of Dionysus, that is, exactly the usual trio, as on the relief from Piraeus (pl. 3). The actor above left, with an ornamented costume and long embroidered sleeves, holds the mask, crowned with a tiara, of the barbarian king whom he has played on the stage. His dress is in no way different from that of contemporary tragedy. However surprising this may be, it agrees with what we know from the language of extant satyr plays.[65] The particular charm of this type of drama lay precisely in the artfully motivated meeting of gods and heroes from the tragic sphere with the altogether different world of the satyrs, who here always formed the chorus. In these young horse-tailed members of the chorus, youthful wild spirits and bold pugnacity were combined with the timid disposition and the stubborn grace of foals. With such a chorus, in spite of the tragic mood of the gods and heroes, the drama could not end in tragedy.

Of the trio of actors on the Naples vase, the one who stands on the right of Dionysus' couch holding the mask and attributes of Heracles is especially prominent. His long sleeves and the fine *kothornoi* decorated with Lydian splendour contrast strangely with the breast-plate, which was probably made of metal. Next to him a young girl is seated on the couch of Dionysus, wearing long sleeves but no *kothornoi* and holding up a female mask, which has always been regarded as that of the title role of the play. This role must have been played by one of the three actors in the picture, probably the one with the mask of the barbarian king. It is the only female mask in the picture, a round face, painted entirely white, in contrast to the masks of the three male roles which are painted yellow.[66] All four correspond with the style of mask of about 400 BC (see pl. 4,2).

Since the title-role mask on the Naples *crater* has a tiara, it must belong to a barbarian princess and, in view of her youthful features and flowing long hair, probably not the wife but the daughter of the barbarian king who stands on the left of the couch. The names of both these roles are unfortunately not recorded, and the suggestion has been made that the action concerned the fate of Hesione, the daughter of the Trojan King Laomedon, who was rescued from a sea monster by

Heracles. But in view of the Eros, who kneels next to the young girl with the mask of the leading role, there must be a love story involved (which is typical of the satyr play), and since this does not occur in the myth of Hesione another barbarian princess must be intended. This really only leaves the Lydian Omphale, and Heracles with Omphale is known to have formed the theme of several satyr plays and comedies of the fifth century BC.[67] Moreover, it is particularly characteristic of Greek dramatists constantly to give fresh interpretations to certain subjects. The Omphale theme was very popular in Athens, because the effeminacy of the Dorian hero Heracles at the Lydian palace of King Iardanos and his daughter, the beautiful Omphale, gave the pretext for funny situations. The exchange of clothes and attributes between Heracles and Omphale is known from representations in Hellenistic and Roman art. This possibly goes back to a satyr play about Omphale, for the exchange of clothes, above all between men and women, was naturally a favourite device in both satyr play and comedy.[68] Besides, in these representations Heracles and Omphale as lovers are nearly always surrounded by the Dionysiac *thiasos*. The Lydians were famous for their cult of Dionysus (a chorus of Lydian maenads appeared in Euripides' *Bacchae*), so that this gave the basic motivation for the appearance of satyrs at the palace of Sardis. The Lydians loved and cultivated music, and it is no accident that on the Naples vase the young man Charinos stands with a lyre next to Pronomos. Consequently the poet Demetrius, who is not as well known to us from ancient literature as the piper Pronomos, had chosen for his victorious piece a very effective subject.

It is difficult to name the girl who holds the mask of the leading heroine next to Heracles. She appears to be the only person in the picture who sees Dionysus and Ariadne, to whom she is turning and on whose couch she has taken a seat (although admittedly at a significant distance). But to the left of the couch a vine grows between Dionysus and the actor, whose head is turned the other way. Therefore, as in the case of the gods on the east frieze of the Parthenon, the divine pair are thought of as invisible to the mortals present. The girl with the mask mediates between the divine sphere and that of the actors. In the art of the 'rich style' this task is often performed by personifications, who were divine beings but stood nearer to mortals than to the great gods. The name *Paidia* has recently been convincingly suggested for this girl. It means 'the personification of the play', or more precisely here of the 'satyr play'.[69] For this light-hearted drama, in which actors in tragic dress were contrasted with the boisterous satyrs, was called by ancient critics τραϑῳδία παίϟουσα, 'playful tragedy'.[70] On a calyx *crater* by the Talos painter,[71] which shows an equally rich figure scene, a banquet of Dionysus with Hephaestus is portrayed, with a silenos dressed as a *kitharodes* playing the *kithara* (pl. 8,1 and reconstruction fig. 2). The young flute player shown near the *kline*, on which a bearded Dionysus reclines, is a satyr named Mimus. He accompanies the dance, which the Greeks called *mimesis*, 'imitation' (cf. p. 29). The banquet takes place under the leaves of a vine (fig. 2), which was still a characteristic stage set for the satyr play during the Hellenistic period (cf. pl. 11,1). The drama represented on this recently acquired Würzburg fragment probably bore the title *Hephaestus*, which is attributed to the satyric playwright Achaeus.[72] The purpose of the banquet was for Dionysus to trick Hephaestus, the drunken blacksmith, whom he had brought back to Olympus in order to free Hera from the magic throne to which she was fastened. The presence of the statue of Athena has not been explained.

Stage painting

The staging of Archaic tragedies down to and including the early tetralogies of Aeschylus was very simple. A tent, a tomb, an altar or several sacred objects of this kind sufficed to indicate the setting.[73]

Fig. 2 Reconstruction drawing of the symposium under a vine which is shown on the fragmentary calyx krater by the Talos painter (Pl. 8.), Würzburg, Martin von Wagner Museum. Drawing (with improvements) from *Pantheon* 36, 1978, 200, fig. 1a.

Siegfried Melchinger speaks convincingly of a 'rock set', which simply consisted of the rocky landscape of the theatre of Dionysus.[74] The set pieces in most cases were probably made of wood. They were stored, one assumes, in the *skene*, the wooden stage-building on the edge of the orchestra. The satyr play appears to have managed throughout the whole of the fifth century with such simple set pieces, to which was added the 'cave', particularly popular in plays of this type.[75] It formed, for example, the background in the partly preserved *Ichneutae* (*Hunting Dogs*) of Sophocles and in Euripides' *Cyclops*. As the satyrs belonged to nature in the wild, the cave was very appropriate. However, it should not be understood as a piece of scenery in our sense, particularly as only its rock-framed entrance was visible. It corresponded to the door of the palace or temple in the middle of the stage building in other plays.[76] What occurred in the interior of the cave, such as the murder of Odysseus' two companions by Polyphemus, was invisible to the spectators and had to be narrated to them. A rocky landscape, in the sense of a transformation of the whole *skene*, postulated by many scholars, must certainly be excluded from the 'cave dramas' of the fifth century.[77] The rocky scenery was limited rather to the surroundings of the cave entrance.

In the fourth century BC this must in principle still have been the case, as an Apulian calyx *crater* recently acquired by the Berlin Museum shows.[78] Its main picture is the only representation of Aeschylus' *Prometheus* so far known in vase painting, and concerns Prometheus' release by Heracles in the second play.[79] The bound Titan stands in an archway built of rock. It is the old cave entrance which can be justified here for technical reasons of staging. For since the Greek stage had no curtain, Prometheus (who was bound motionless for thousands of years) must have been wheeled out on the *ekkyklema* through a door in the *skene*.[80] Because of the mountain in the myth of Prometheus this door was represented as a rocky entrance. Moreover it had here another meaning, as the door of Tartarus, into which Prometheus was plunged by Zeus' thunderbolt at the end of the first part of the trilogy. This action was portrayed on the stage not vertically but horizontally, by rolling back the *ekkyklema* behind the rocky entrance, which had already formed the background of the first play.

As in the case of Prometheus, Andromeda must have been shown on the *ekkyklema*, bound to a rock, at the start of Euripides' tragedy of that name which was first performed in 412 BC.[81] Here too a cave entrance formed the background, and this often appears on South Italian vases behind the heroine on the sea-shore.[82] Euripides has ingeniously incorporated it into the action, by making the nymph

Echo live in the cave, and listen to the bound Andromeda's mono-
logue at the beginning of the tragedy. This episode shows particularly
clearly how the limited technical resources of the Attic stage did not
hamper the dramatists, but rather inspired their creative imagination.
The same is true of the officially fixed limitation of the actors to three,
which did not harm Attic drama but gave it an unrivalled intensity.

The Euripidean *Andromeda* was preceded by a tragedy of the same
name by Sophocles, written in the mid-fifth century. We would know
little about it, since the scanty fragments hardly give anything away, if
we did not have a series of Attic vase paintings.[83] On these the king's
daughter is not, as in Euripides' play, bound to a rock, but to a stake;
and she was not shown on the *ekkyklema*, but was brought forward
and bound before the spectators' eyes. It appeared that in this drama
Sophocles wanted if possible to avoid rocky stage sets. And yet no less
a witness than Aristotle names this dramatist as the one who introduced stage painting, σκηνογραφία (*Poetics* I449a). How is that to be
understood?

What the Greeks called *skenographia* had nothing to do with
landscape painting. It was rather the representation of architecture in
perspective. It was called stage painting because Greek artists had
discovered the possibility of foreshortening architectural forms
through painting the flat panels which were attached to the stage-
building. Sophocles must have introduced scene painting in perspective towards 460 BC at the latest, for his older rival Aeschylus, who
was particularly devoted to innovations on the stage, also used this
invention. According to Vitruvius Aeschylus employed the painter
Agatharchus of Samos to paint a perspective stage set, of which the
artist left a written account. Stimulated by him, Democritus and
Anaxagoras wrote, on the same subject,[84] that

> according to a natural law lines must correspond with the gaze of
> the eyes and the rectilinear extension of the beams, once a
> particular position is established as middle point; so that ... clear
> pictures can reproduce the appearance of buildings in stage-scenery,
> and that which is painted on vertical and flat surfaces appears to be
> partly receding and partly advancing.

The most important surviving imitation of a stage set in vase
painting is found on the fragment of a calyx *crater* in Würzburg, which
was painted in the middle of the fourth century BC in Tarentum
(pl. 10, and reconstruction figs. 3; 4).[85]

The Tarentines of that late classical period were so fond of the
theatre that it is not surprising that one of their vase painters had the
idea of copying a perspective stage set known to him from the theatre.

Fig. 3 Reconstruction of the Würzburg *skenographia* partially illustrated in
Pl. 10 (drawing by B. Otto). The maeander motif base in the 1972 edition has
been replaced by an egg pattern at A.D. Trendall's suggestion. It is typical of
the Konnakis Group, cf. AA, 1973, 125, fig. 3.

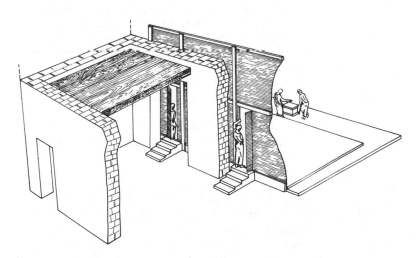

Fig. 4 Reconstruction of the stage-building which is faced by the *skenographia*
of fig. 3 (drawing by B. Otto), cf. AA, 1973, 129, fig. 5.

In his publication of the Würzburg *skene* painting, Heinrich Bulle assumed that the vase painter wanted to reproduce a real stage-building with wings projecting on each side. But such is the magnificence of this architecture (it has golden *acroteria* and gold on the coffering of the ceiling, which is shown in foreshortening as lozenges, but is really rectangular), that one could hardly think of a real building. The Greeks did not yet have the grandiose façade of the *scaenae frons*, which would not have been sufficiently adaptable for their ideas of drama, but they disguised the simple stage-building with architectural pictures painted in perspective. Such a painting, which includes 'real' doors (as in our modern stage sets),[86] is intended on the Würzburg fragment. Female figures stand in the two doorways: the left hand one, which is better preserved, is reproduced here (pl. 10). As they appear further back, these girls are smaller than the two male figures in the foreground. What is particularly interesting about this picture is that all four figures are correctly proportioned in relation to the architecture. Although they are not wearing masks they must be intended as actors in a tragedy: Tarentine vase painters, like Attic ones, often omitted the masks. The subject is probably the arrival of Jason in Iolcus, at the court of the king, Pelias, who is shown making an offering from a golden cup. This was Bulle's interpretation, and if it is correct Jason must have been painted with only one shoe, in accordance with the myth. Unfortunately this part is not preserved, nor is the low altar on which the aged Pelias poured his libation. It must have been a solid 'prop', in contrast to the grandiose portico of the royal palace (in which the two daughters of Pelias are eavesdropping) which is only painted. These daughters will later be persuaded by Medea to cause their father's death, and this misfortune has its origin here in the meeting with Jason. A play entitled *Peliades* is attested for Euripides, and Sophocles treated the subject in his *Rhizotomoi* (*The Collectors of Magic Roots*).[87]

There is only one piece comparable to the Würzburg stage set: the picture on a Campanian bell *crater* in the Louvre, of about the same period.[88] This shows a scene from Euripides' *Iphigenia in Tauris*. Here again a building with two wings is portrayed, although without such skill in perspective as on the Würzburg painting. Here too a folding door, of which evidently only one wing was 'real', opens on the left and right sides.[89] In the lefthand doorway stands the Taurian Artemis, and from the righthand one Iphigenia comes out to speak to Orestes and Pylades. As with the Würzburg fragment, scholars have here thought that the architecture was actually constructed, that is, they have assumed a stage-building with *paraskenia* jutting out on either side. This has raised the problem that in both cases only two lateral doors were used, whereas the central door, which according to the interpretation of many scholars was sufficient for classical drama, was missing.[90] But if we reckon that both vase paintings represent not actual, but painted, architecture the hypothesis of the central door is saved.

It appears that in the discussion about the number of doors on the classical stage, an important passage in Pollux (4.124) has not received sufficient attention. It would not be doing justice to it if one were to explain the three doors which he attests for the stage-building simply in terms of the *scaenae frons* of the Imperial period (Pollux wrote his *Onomastikon* for Prince Commodus, the son of Marcus Aurelius). As is well known, the author elsewhere only gives information about Greek, and moreover specifically Attic, matters and not about Roman Imperial ones. By his motto 'the minimum possible and theatrical practice are two separate things', Newiger has convincingly defended the use of three doors in the stage-building of the last quarter of the fifth century.[91] He takes Aristophanic comedy as his starting point, and observes, with reference to the *didaskalos* (producer) who trained the tragic chorus, that he did not need 'to make do with the absolutely necessary minimum of a single door'. Now Pollux tells us in the passage mentioned above that in tragic productions one of the three doors, the lefthand one, remained closed. This is evidence for two real doors in tragedy, the same number which appears in the two tragic scene paintings discussed above. This correlation does not seem to me coincidental. The view that after a certain point, still to be determined, in the fifth century tragedians had the use of two doors, which they did not always need to use, can be laid down as a basic working assumption for future interpretations of stage production.

The painted backdrop which a gifted Campanian mural artist copied around 50 BC, in a bedroom in the Villa of Boscoreale near Vesuvius, originates in the Hellenistic period (pl. 11).[92] The decoration of the whole room is now in the Metropolitan Museum, New York. Here we reproduce only two sections, whose high rectangular form, however, corresponds with the shape of the original. It differs from the long rectangle of the scene paintings discussed above, because the Hellenistic stage was differently built.[93] The stage-building no longer had the simple wall, disguised by an architectural painting attached to it, but it was divided architecturally as a 'façade'. The scenery consisted of several partial views only, which were set into the openings (*thyromata*) in the façade.[94] Thereby the step was taken to the *scaenae frons*, which usually still showed *thyromata* for scenery in the earlier Imperial period.[95] The variously constructed scenes from the *cubiculum* (bedroom) of Boscoreale have been convincingly connected with a passage in Vitruvius (5.6.9), which says:

> There are three types of scene, one of which is called tragic, the second comic, the third satyric. Their decoration is very different. The tragic scenes are constructed of columns, pediments, statues and other things which belong to the royal palace. Comic scenes have a view of private houses, bay windows and projecting rooms with windows, as in real houses. Satyric scenes, however, are decorated with trees, grottoes, hills and other rustic things, in the manner of a landscape picture.

Here we do not reproduce the tragic scenery of Boscoreale, which portrays sanctuaries of Artemis and Aphrodite, but part of the probable comic and satyric scenery.

Comic decoration (which in the Hellenistic period naturally refers to that of New Comedy) consists, like tragic, of architecture painted in perspective (that is, *skenographia*). In pl. 11,2 even the bay window which Vitruvius mentions as typical of comic scenery can be seen on the right, above the magnificent false door. On its roof stands a broken pot with a plant in it, which certainly allows a closer identification of the play to which the decoration belongs. The drama took place in a town which had just celebrated the festival of Adonis, when the women put broken pots containing various kinds of plants on the roof of the house. As we know from the newly-discovered *Samia* of Menander, the festival of Adonis was a familiar setting for plots in New Comedy.[96] Since the festival was also and above all sacred to Aphrodite, the comic scenery of Boscoreale is a fitting counterpart to the temple of Aphrodite in the tragic stage set. Both styles of decoration are also suitable, from this point of view, for a bedroom. The finishing touches to this work are provided by the satyric scenery, which is immediately next to the bed (pl. 11,1). The airy bower, cool grotto and splashing fountain exhibit the typical elements of the *locus amoenus*[97] which Ernst Robert Curtius discovered in ancient literature, and which also reappears constantly in ancient landscape painting. In such a spot, beside the goddess of love, gentle sleep reigns above all, *somnus agrestium lenis virorum* (Horace, *Odes* 3.I.21f.). As the spring is not mentioned among the items which Vitruvius lists as comprising satyric scenery, many scholars have wanted to remove it from the original stage set, but surely wrongly. The artificially built fountain seems to me more probably to point to a particular play. The satyr play *Amymone* by Aeschylus, who was regarded in ancient times as the best composer of satyric drama, had as the focus of its plot a spring, near which the eponymous heroine fell asleep when fetching water, was molested by satyrs, and finally became the beloved of her rescuer Poseidon.[98] The fountain concerned had three streams, created by the trident of the god; and the fountain in our picture has three water-spouts. It gives away the name of the satyr play for us, especially as the spring kept the name Amymone (Hyginus, *Fabulae* 169).

The Hellenistic painter, who reconstructed this charming portrait of nature, has completely reshaped the old theatrical 'cave' motif. The rocks here certainly surrounded an entrance which led into the interior of the stage-building, but this is concealed with great refinement, in contrast to the simple cave entrances of the classical period. The copyist of Boscoreale has probably taken this game of hide-and-seek even further by the way he trails the tendrils of ivy. His stylistic devices certainly have nothing to do with classical stage sets from which many scholars wished to derive the basic form of the painting. By means of the vine arbour and the fountain, which is painted in perspective, the landscape picture is united with the *skenographia* in a mixed form which is typical of Hellenistic art.

Despite the difference of style between the classical stage set and the Hellenistic one at Boscoreale, there is a connection. Compare the wing of the portico on the Würzburg fragment (pl. 10) with the arbour in the satyric scenery (pl. 11,1). In both cases the viewpoint is set equally low down: the view upwards to the coffered ceiling is paralleled by the view up to the lightly trellised roof. Boscoreale's other stage sets also have this low viewpoint. This may have been from the first an artistic device to allow the actors not to appear too small, and if so it probably even contributed to the invention of perspective scenery. The style was certainly at its most popular during the fifth and fourth centuries, since at that time it affected the whole length of the *skene* (stage-building). On the Hellenistic stage, where it served only to fill the *thyromata* in individual scenes, it lost some of its significance. Nevertheless the Hellenistic period also had excellent and original stage sets, which are echoed in the frescoes of Boscoreale.

Old Comedy, Phlyax farce, New Comedy

Comedy was the last dramatic genre to be admitted to the festival programme of the 'Great Dionysia' at Athens.[99] It was first performed there during the Persian Wars, and from then on Old Comedy, which found its master in Aristophanes, developed as a literary form. Its pre-literary period, however, was longer than in the case of tragedy and the satyr play, and archaeologically also it can be traced further back. At any rate a greater wealth of pictorial evidence is preserved for this genre than for the other two, since comedy was far more popular. One need only think of the innumerable terracottas, from the classical to the late periods, which portray actors in comedy or comic masks (pl. 12).[100] The small figures were found in tombs, which at first might seem astonishing, and which must imply that comedy was deeply rooted in religion. The clay figures had prehistoric origins: as is well known, prehistoric tribes which developed agriculture and a settled life left behind numerous idols with thick bellies and backsides, many of which are female, but others clearly male.[101] This prehistoric physique was shown on the stage of the classical period by actors of Old and Middle Comedy, who performed with padded bellies and backsides. Padding was compulsory for all roles, men and women, spirits and gods. Costume and stage props were added to this grotesque basic shape in accordance with the role. The most important attribute for male roles was a big, artificial phallus, which appeared from under the short dress. It belonged to the origins of comedy, which according to Aristotle's evidence (*Poetics* I449a) was created and developed from the phallus songs, which were still sung in his time in many places during the winter festival of the 'Rural Dionysia'.[102] In the *Acharnians* Aristophanes has portrayed a procession in which a phallus symbol was carried on stage and addressed in song (242ff.).

In Menander's 'New Comedy' decency was respected: the actors of male roles, like those of female roles, were clothed in long costumes and the padding of belly and backside was eliminated.[103] It is a phenomenon which deserves further consideration that in the classical period the grotesque, phallic, comic actors could appear at the same festival and in honour of the same god as tragic performers. It shows the flexibility of the drama and the open-mindedness of the public in the fifth and fourth centuries, a tolerance which disappeared after the early Hellenistic period.

The Archaic 'padded dancers' were previously regarded by literary and archaeological scholars as forerunners of Old Comedy, until they were wrongly identified by Ernst Buschor and his school as early satyrs.[104] But, as is now generally recognized, their dress survives in comedy rather than in the satyr play. Each wears a short jacket, under which the belly and backside is thickly padded (fig. 5). The jacket should not be interpreted as clothing, but as 'skin'; T. B. L. Webster aptly speaks of 'dramatic skin'.[105] His theory that the origin of all three types of drama lay in the dances of these grotesque companies is, however, contradicted by the fact that the Greeks had too strong a consciousness of the independence and incompatibility of literary genres. As we have seen, satyr play and tragedy are indeed related, but comedy is separated from both by an unbridgeable gap. It was autonomous and had its own poets, and, according to Aristotle, its own origin, separate from that of tragedy. It is true that the different types of drama served to honour Dionysus; but this god, like other great gods, united in his personality strong contrasts, which were also expressed in the form of his cult. The Classical period, more than any other, could assimilate these contrasts.

An argument in favour of renaming the 'padded dancers' as satyrs has been seen in the fact that many of these grotesque figures bore the names of spirits, as perhaps shown on a Corinthian *krater* of the early sixth century BC (fig. 5).[106] But the names written next to them, Eunos ('well disposed'), and Ophelandros ('helpful to men') sound different from the names of satyrs familiar to us. Roland Hampe has shown, in contrast to older interpretations,[107] that all the figures in this scene are seized by the rhythm of a dance. They are acting out in dancing (Greek *mimesis*)[108] the problems of carrying a full *krater*. A double-pipe player is also present dressed in the padded jacket (fig. 5; cf. pl. 1). In front of him dances a man with a long beard, thus characterized as older than the others. He does not wear a mask as was supposed. It is a vulgar dance, possibly the *kordax*,[109] a solo dance which was performed especially by the drunk and elderly — both men and women. It was as typical of comedy as the *sikinnis* was of satyr play. These dances were no more interchangeable than was the appearance of their dancers, for while the *sikinnis* with its bold leaps accorded with the satyrs' equine nature, the vulgar *kordax* suited the grotesque but purely human form of the padded dancers. From these dances, it should be emphasized once more, there is no way leading to satyr play and tragedy, but there is probably a direct path to Old Comedy.

Fig. 5 Padded dancers with a flute player. Black-figure vase painting, Corinth, c. 600 BC, Paris, Louvre E 632. From M. Bieber, *Die Denkmäler zum Theater-wesen im Altertum* (Berlin, 1920), n. 72b.

As the grotesque spirits which were imitated in dance go back to a very early period, they obviously did not belong only to Dionysus. In the prehistoric period female deities were predominant, and then in the historical period grotesque forms were encountered in the cults of Demeter as well as those of Artemis.[110] Artemis sometimes appears on Corinthian vases with 'padded dancers', and according to literary sources played a part in the origin of comedy. The goddess concerned was the Doric Artemis, worshipped in Sparta and Corinth and·in the Doric colonies of South Italy and Sicily. That pre-literary comedy arose in Doric areas is explicitly attested; even the step towards literary comedy was completed there earlier than in other areas: as Aristotle observed, the Sicilian comic poet Epicharmus precedes the earliest Attic victors in comedy (*Poetics* 1448a). The most important source for early Doric comedy is to be found in Athenaeus (14.621), where the theft of crops, or treatment by some foreign quack, are said to have been 'imitated in a light style of speech'. This passage has always been rightly connected with the Corinthian *crater* mentioned above (fig. 5), on whose other side is shown the punishment of two thieves who have broken into a strongroom and are now confined in the stocks.[111] Since a flute player is shown on the other side it is certain that we are dealing here with an 'imitation', that is to say a dramatic performance.

In the same passage Athenaeus names the actors in such farces, which varied from place to place and thereby indicates their popularity. In Sicyon near Corinth, for example, they were called *phallophoroi*, and this agrees with the evidence of Aristotle that comedy developed from phallic songs. In Italy they were called *phlyakes*. We know *phlyakes* from many fourth-century Italian vase paintings (pl. 14).[112] In these pictures the old Doric farce frequently lives on, as for example on the calyx *crater* by the Paestan painter, Assteas, which is illustrated here and is in the Berlin-Charlottenburg museum. On this vase two thieves are pulling the old man Charinos off his money chest, while his servant stands by trembling helplessly. The four actors still wear the old stuffed jacket of the 'padded dancers'. Charinos and his servant are also clothed in short, white chitons, but the thieves are supposed to appear naked, although the 'skin' on their arms and legs consists of a brownish costume, and on their torsos of a dark red one, on which nipples and navel are painted. Such contrasts increased the comic effect.

Besides the Doric themes in the *phlyax* pieces we may also detect a strong Attic influence, which originated in Aristophanes' Old Comedy. Attic tragedy had itself influenced the *phlyakes*, in the sense that they parodied the myths which were shaped by tragedy.[113] In this respect Aristophanes was the innovator, with his parodies of situations in Euripides' tragedies. An original example of the equal influence of both tragedy and comedy on early *phlyax* themes is to be found on an Apulian *crater* painted *c.* 370 BC and now in Würzburg (pl. 15).[114] The Mysian king, Telephos, kneels on an altar with his 'hostage' who is not the child Orestes, but rather a wine skin (*askos*). The nurse will collect the child's 'blood', as in Aristophanes' *Thesmophoriazusae* (689ff.) in which Euripides' *Telephos* is parodied. The small shoes, which disguise the wine skin, also tally with this. Local Italian influences must also have played a part in these *phlyax* farces, especially in the language. We can gauge these influences from the fragments of Rhinthon of Syracuse, who lived in the early third century BC, of whose work unfortunately only a few fragments are preserved. He is mentioned in ancient sources as the first poet of the *phlyakes*, which is astonishing since the majority of Italian vases with *phlyax* themes (a survey of which was published by A.D. Trendall) belong to the fourth century BC.[115] This problem can be solved: as the similarities between *phlyax* vases and the themes of Rhinthon show, he must have been the first to record many early comedies in writing. Thus, in the Italian *phlyax* farces, the pre-literary period of old Attic comedy is revived at a much later stage. It is well known that Aristophanes portrayed comic choruses of animals and riders — Frogs, Wasps, Birds and Knights, for example — but as Attic black-figure vase paintings show such choruses already appeared in Archaic comedy some hundred years before Aristophanes.[116] If we did not have the archaeological evidence, the pre-literary stages of Old Comedy (as of *phlyax* farces) would have been unknown to us.

The animal choruses of Aristophanes go back even earlier than the Archaic period. Their origins are ultimately rooted in prehistoric religion, like the grotesque shapes of the 'padded dancers'. Artemis the 'mistress of animals', who played her part in the development of comedy, had 'bees' or 'bears' among the servants of her cult from the earliest period, that is to say, people who identified themselves with these creatures in the service of the goddess. Because their origin lies in the pre-literary period we cannot say when animal choruses first appeared in comedies. It is only certain that they were not indispensable, as was the satyr chorus in the satyr play. The chorus of comedy could equally well be composed of 'padded dancers'. The animal choruses, however, together with the versatile language which ranged from vulgar jokes to the realms of lyric poetry, gave to Old Comedy a variety and an imaginative scope which no other dramatic genre possessed.

While the *phlyakes* were still in command of the comic stage in South Italy and Sicily, Athens, which since the late Archaic period had been the centre of dramatic innovation, produced an entirely new form of entertainment: New Comedy. Its poets formed, like the classical tragedians, a triumvirate (Philemon, Diphilos, Menander), of whom (despite his short career) Menander has enjoyed the highest fame in the judgement of posterity. His work has become more familiar to us in recent times as a result of papyrus discoveries in Egypt. To these have been added the archaeological evidence from the late antique mosaics of Mytilene on Lesbos, which illustrate eleven of Menander's comedies.[117] Here, in contrast to classical or Archaic vase paintings, one can really speak of illustrations to a text, for the mosaics reproduce definite passages in the plays, as their inscriptions show. The scenes belong to a tradition of illustrations incorporated with the texts which began in the Hellenistic period, continued in the Roman period, survived the Middle Ages and acquired a new life in the Renaissance.[118] At that time illustrations to the plays of Terence, who together with Plautus had established New Comedy in Rome, were the most popular.

Here only a single comedy may be selected from the mosaics of Lesbos, a scene which shows with three women seated at a table eating. The composition was already known from one of Dioscurides' two famous mosaics from Pompeii (pl. 13).[119] Friedrich Marx and, following him, T.B.L. Webster suggested that it portrays the opening scene of Menander's *Women Breakfasting Together* (*Synaristosai*). The mosaic in Mytilene confirms this. We are looking into an interior, which is very rare in ancient staging. It was opened for the spectator by a *thyroma* in the wall of the *skene*. The effect must have resembled our stage-box. Moreover, the various vertical and horizontal bands on the left and top sides, which are distinguished by different colours, resemble our own stage convention.[120] Probably the *thyroma* was closed before the beginning of the play, and was then opened to give an unfamiliar view into the women's dining room. The successful comic effect must have thus been ensured even before the first verses were spoken. Plautus uses the same recipe at the beginning of his *Cistellaria*. The late antique mosaic gives us the original names, which have been altered in Plautus. The old woman is called Philainis, opposite her sits Pythias, and in the middle Plangon. The little servant-girl who stands at the far right is a nameless mute role. The mask of the old woman, with a full but wrinkled face, has its counterpart in a terracotta mask in the Martin von Wagner Museum in Würzburg (pl. 12.1).[121] In the mosaic it is yellowish with squinting eyes and white hair, round which her mantle is wrapped. It emerges from the *Cistellaria* that she is a bawd (*lena*). The *hetaira* Pythias, sitting opposite her, is her daughter. Both are being entertained by Plangon, who plays the role of a false maiden

(*Pseudokorē*). As her gestures show Plangon is engaged in a lively con-versation with the old woman. Pythias listens and, to while away the time, lets a string of beads slip through her fingers. These are the 'worry beads' (κομπολόγι), which enjoyed great popularity with ancient *hetairai* and are still known today in the Balkans and in the Middle East.[122] The mask of Pythias, with the band in the full hair, can be compared with an impressive terracotta mask in the Martin von Wagner Museum (pl. 12,2 and cover picture).

The original of the Dioscurides mosaic dates from the early third century BC, like both clay masks. The three women wear the early Hellenistic female costume. Their bodies are no longer padded as in Old Comedy, and the rather stiff shape of Pythias makes it clear that the *hetaira* is played by a man. The contemporary costume, prevalent in New Comedy, is supplemented by a typical theatrical property — the long added sleeves. These sleeves are not only typical for actors, but also for Thalia, the comic Muse, in Roman representations. As the other mosaic of Dioscurides from Pompeii shows, they could be simply white, indicating skin (like the white face of the mask) as we have conjectured above for the sleeves of tragic actors. From the recent discovery in Mytilene, this mosaic can also be identified as illustrating Menander's *Theophoroumene* (*Possessed Woman*).[123] The find has shown how with the help of new material a whole series of old problems can be solved and theories confirmed. Our understanding of the ancient theatre cannot progress without questions and theories. One hopes that new archaeological finds, like that at Lesbos, or new interpreta-tions of known material, will contribute further to the solution of such problems.

The Roman theatre

For the literary problems connected with the Roman theatre the reader is referred to the comprehensive work by Eckart Lefèvre.[124] The archaeological problems are only discussed here in a brief summary.

The oldest purely Roman theatre which is preserved lies to the southeast of the large theatre at Pompeii which was built in the Hellenistic period.[125] The small building, for 1500 spectators, was erected soon after the refoundation of Pompeii by Sulla in 80 BC. The orchestra was reduced to a semicircle and in addition was made much smaller by the addition of several rows of flat steps on which the portable seats of honour could be placed. The rows of seats which were thus added are correspondingly shorter on the side, since the semicircle of the *cavea* is trimmed so that it fits into a rectangle. This angular shape is certainly not mirrored in all Roman theatres, but is probably more typical of the *theatrum tectum* or *odeum*, the concert hall. For the Pompeian building, which even today in its ruined state gives an impression of compactness and unity, had a permanent roof, whereas for technical reasons the large Roman theatre, laid out in a semicircle, did not have a permanent roof; but it may well have had an awning, like the amphitheatres designed for animal fights and gladiatorial games (cf. note 24).

There was no stone theatre in Rome itself until the late Republic. The numerous performances took place on movable stages, which were influenced by the South Italian *phlyakes'* wooden stages (cf. pl. 14).[126] The first stone theatre in Rome was dedicated by Pompey in 55 BC. The magnificent building situated on the Campus Martius was indeed used down to late antiquity, but today its site can only be established by the layout of the streets in that area.[127] On the other hand, in the case of the nearby theatre of Marcellus, dedicated by Augustus in 11 BC, two storeys of the exterior façade of the auditorium can still be seen. The *cavea* and the *scaenae frons*, as with Pompey's theatre and all other subsequent Roman theatre buildings, were here united in a permanent architectural structure. The theatre of Marcellus served as the model for countless similar buildings in the

Roman world. It also had an influence on the exterior arrangement of the amphitheatre, exemplified in the Colosseum in Rome.

The Augustan period was not only influential in theatre building, but also produced the last type of ancient drama, the pantomime or *fabula saltica*,[128] which continued to be performed until the Byzantine period. It should not be confused with the older mime, a broad maskless farce which was acted with dancing or acrobatic intermezzos and belonged to the sphere of comedy. For the new genre soon confined itself to the domain of tragedy; comic pantomimes soon appear to have lost their importance, so that one can see the pantomime as a substitute for the declining tragedy. The adaptation was done in such a way that the most significant and effective parts of the action were put together in a series of lyric solo acts, performed by a pantomime actor, who therefore had to act an ever-increasing number of roles, both male and female, in succession while the text appropriate to each solo was sung by a whole chorus, and not by one singer as in drama proper.

One might suppose that, in pantomime, drama had reverted to its Archaic form, the chorus with a single actor, were it not for the fact that everything else had been changed. For the chorus did not dance in the orchestra, indeed it generally did not dance at all and was also unseen. Stationed behind a screen (or 'Spanish wall'), it sang an accompaniment to the dancing of the solo pantomime actor, on whom the spectators' whole attention was concentrated. In view of such solo performances it is no wonder that pantomime actors could develop into 'stars' in our modern sense. Like the creators of this type of drama, the Cilician Pylades and the Alexandrian Bathyllus, they usually came from the Hellenized Greek East, the source of the great majority of Imperial actors. The bodies of the pantomime actors, for whom the name Paris is several times attested, had to be faultless and capable of great variety of expression, since they portrayed all roles by artistic balletic movements only, without saying a word. So the mouth of the mask which they wore on their heads was also shut, in contrast to the gaping mouth of tragic and comic masks (pl. 4; 12; 16).[129] Until recently only late pantomimic masks were attested, but I should like to believe that recent finds represent early Augustan masks of this type, thus dating from the period of the origins of the *fabula saltica*.

Several grand rooms have recently been excavated on the Palatine near the 'House of Livia', which have received the collective name of 'House of Augustus'.[130] Such a designation is not too much to assume, for the imperial family must actually have lived there. The decoration belongs to the later phase of the 'second style' (30-20 BC), and, in the room which is particularly lavish in its decoration, the theme is the *scaenae frons*. The wings of the main door (*valvae regiae*, cf. Vitruvius 5, 7) are missing. Instead we look on an idyllic landscape with a shrine of Apollo — Augustus' main deity.[131] This backdrop is painted with hazy soft colours, which stand in effective contrast to the vigorously colourful stage architecture. Between the 'king's door' and the two side doors (*hospitalia*) on the right and left, are screen walls hung with masks. They cannot directly be classed among the known types of tragic and comic masks. The form is on the whole close to the tragic one, but the shut mouth appears to smile mischievously, and the expressively rolling eyes lack the slanting 'Laocoon's brows', which are typical of the tragic masks of the Imperial period. Hence these are probably masks for the actors in an early *fabula saltica*. The theme of the piece may be Apolline, and to this the middle picture refers. Thus, a comparable pantomime wall painting of the 'fourth style' from Pompeii alludes to the theme of 'Apollo and Marsyas'.[132] One can conclude from the singers who stand behind the side screens in this painting that the corresponding walls in the stage decoration of 'Augustus' house' are to be conceived as a camouflage for the chorus. From there, invisible to the public, the chorus accompanied in song the solo dance of the pantomime actor.

Screens such as these, but also different forms of drops, were a characteristic of the Roman stage. The small drops (*siparia*) resemble our blinds and were similarly drawn upwards. They served to conceal some parts of the stage. But the whole stage could have been covered by a large curtain, the *aulaeum*. At the start of the play this curtain was not lifted, as on our stage, but was lowered and let into a channel in the floor. This slot is preserved in many Roman theatres.[133] The theatre curtains themselves have not survived, but as we know from Ovid's *Metamorphoses* (3, 111ff.) and Virgil's *Georgics* (3, 25ff.), they could be decorated with figures. As Servius wrote on the above passage of Virgil, the name *aulaeum* originated 'ab aula Attali regis, in qua primum inventa sunt vela ingentia'. Curtains which could be lowered were known not only in the Attalid court at Pergamon but also in the court of the Seleucids in Syria, as is shown by the purple curtain behind Zeus' statue in the temple at Olympia, which was dedicated by Antiochus (Paus. 5, 12, 4). For the use of this device on the stage, however, Virgil is our earliest literary evidence.

While the pantomime's burlesque of tragic themes relegated tragedy proper to the background, New Comedy was maintained through the centuries on the Roman stage in the form which Plautus and Terence had given it.[134] Since the action of these plays was set in the Greek world, and they were performed by actors clad in Greek costumes, they belonged to the sphere of the *fabula palliata* (from *pallium*, the

Greek *himation*). In contrast to them was the *fabula togata* (in native Roman dress), which however did not attain particular significance either as comedy or as tragedy. One of the reasons for this was the fact that topical themes were hardly tolerated on the stage in tragic or comic form during the Imperial period. However, the deeper cause lay in the dramatic strength of the mythology shaped by the classical tragedians, which was maintained down to the Byzantine period.

Notes

This short survey owes its inspiration chiefly to the works of Margarete Bieber, Sir A. Pickard-Cambridge and T.B.L. Webster. Three of these authors' works which are most often cited will be abbreviated as follows:

Bieber, *History* = M. Bieber, *The History of the Greek and Roman Theater* (Princeton, 1961).
Pickard-Cambridge, *DFA* = A. Pickard-Cambridge, *The Dramatic Festivals of Athens* (2nd edn, Oxford, 1968).
Webster, *GTP* = T.B.L. Webster, *Greek Theatre Production* (2nd edn, London, 1970).

Since the completion of the manuscript for the first edition of 1972, a series of works on the subject has appeared, a selection of which is cited here:

Blume = H.D. Blume, *Einführung in das antike Theaterwesen* (Darmstadt, 1978).
Ghiron-Bistagne = P. Ghiron-Bistagne, *Recherches sur les acteurs dans la Grèce antique* (Paris, 1976).
Melchinger = S. Melchinger, *Das Theater der Tragödie* (München, 1974).
Newiger = H.-J. Newiger, 'Drama und Theater', in G.A. Seeck, *Das griechische Drama* (Darmstadt, 1979) 434ff.
Snell, *TrGFI* = B. Snell, *Tragicorum Graecorum Fragmenta I* (Göttingen, 1971).
Trendall/Webster = A.D. Trendall and T.B.L. Webster, *Illustrations of Greek Drama* (London, 1971).

1 W. Dörpfeld and E. Reisch, *Das griechische Theater* (Athens, 1896), A. Pickard-Cambridge, *The Theatre of Dionysus in Athens* (Oxford, 1966), J. Travlos (ed.) *Bildlexikon zur Topographie des antiken Athen* (Tübingen, 1971), 537ff. (English edn, *Pictorial Dictionary of Ancient Athens*, London, 1971) and Blume, 45ff.
2 On the Proagon, see Pickard-Cambridge, *DFA*, 67f. The actors appeared wreathed, but without masks and costumes. The Proagon was held, from Pericles' time, in the Odeion which he built in the neighbourhood of the theatre of Dionysus. It is not known where it took place earlier. On the terms 'trilogy' and 'tetralogy' see Pickard-Cambridge, *DFA*, 80f.
3 See A. von Gerkan and W. Müller-Wiener, *Das Theater von Epidauros* (Stuttgart, 1961).

4 The ancient sources concerning Thespis are collected and discussed by A. Pickard-Cambridge, *Dithyramb, Tragedy and Comedy* (2nd edn revised by T.B.L. Webster, Oxford, 1962). Cf. Snell, *TrGFI*, no. 1, 61ff.

5 See Pickard-Cambridge, *DFA*, 239ff.

6 H. Froning, 'Dithyrambos und Vasenmalerei in Athen', *Beiträge zur Archäologie 2* (Würzburg, 1971).

7 See note 1. In Travlos the circular segment which Dörpfeld discovered is regarded as the boundary wall of the sacred precinct. But circular temenos walls are not otherwise attested for archaic sanctuaries. Cf. B. Bergquist, *The Archaic Greek Temenos* (Lund, 1967).

8 On *thymele* see note 1, Dörpfeld and Reisch, 278ff. Recent literature: Pickard-Cambridge, *DFA*, 60 n.7, Blume, 73ff.

9 On the columnar form of this image see E. Simon, M. and A. Hirmer, *Die griechischen Vasen* (Munich, 1976), 212ff. pl. 169. Confirmatory evidence appears in a fragment of Euripides' *Antiope*, as reconstructed by B. Snell. In this tragedy, which takes place in the vicinity of Eleutherai, the cult-pillar of Dionysus, who was worshipped there, is mentioned. See B. Snell, *Szenen aus griechischen Dramen* (Berlin, 1971), 82 n.19.

10 For Sophilos' fragment (Athens, National Museum), see P.E. Arias, B.B. Shefton and M. Hirmer, *A History of Greek Vase Painting* (London, 1962), pl. 39, and Ghiron-Bistagne, 199 fig. 64. On the ἴκρια see Pickard-Cambridge, *The Theatre of Dionysus in Athens* (Oxford, 1946), 11ff.

11 See M. Maass, 'Die Prohedrie des Dionysostheaters in Athen', *Vestigia 15* (Münich, 1972).

12 See Pickard-Cambridge, *DFA*, 263.

13 A recent clear discussion of the form of the stage house in the classical period is in W. Jobst, *Die Höhle im Griechischen Theater des 5 und 4 Jhs. v. Chr.* (Vienna, 1970), 10ff. On this see H. Froning, *Gnomon* 45, 1973, 78ff., also T. Dohrn, *RM*, 84, 1977, 211ff.

14 On the dating of this foundation from conglomerate (breccia) stone in the fourth century, see note 1, Dörpfeld and Reisch, 12f., and Travlos, 537. Against this, see Newiger, 448f., who takes the paraskenia to belong to the second half of the fifth century BC.

15 These excavations are being conducted jointly by the Greeks and Germans.

16 See Bieber, *History*, 76; Webster, *GTP*; 17ff., 173; Melchinger, 192ff. and Newiger, 452ff. See also note 80.

17 See Bieber ibid., Webster, *GTP*, 11f.; Melchinger, 194ff. and Newiger, 451f. For the use of the flying machine by Aeschylus, see also E. Fraenkel, *Der Einzug des Chors im 'Prometheus'. Kleine Beiträge zur klassischen Philologie 1* (Rome, 1964) 389ff.

18 In H.-J. Newiger, 'Retraktationen zu Aristophanes' "Frieden"', *Rhein. Mus.* 108, 1965, 238f. and Newiger, 450f.

19 An idea of false doors as a decorative motif is given by the façade of the early Hellenistic tomb recently discovered in Leukadia. See Ph. Petsas, Ὁ τάφος τῶν Λευκαδίων, (Athens, 1966), pl. A. The visitor to Pompeii will be familiar with the motif of the false door, from the First Style (e.g.

the entrance of the Casa del Fauno), down to the Fourth. Cf. also here pl. 11,2.

20 See note 18, Newiger, 229ff. and references.
21 See E. Fiechter, *Das Theater von Oropos* (Stuttgart, 1930) and Bieber, *History*, 111f.
22 For the difference between the architecture of the Greek and Roman theatre, see the comparison in Bieber, *History*, 189.
23 Th. Kraus, *Das römische Weltreich. Propyläen-Kunstgeschichte II* (1967), pl. 63. See also the recent guide by J.P. Clébert, *Provence Antique II* (Paris, 1970), 226f.
24 R. Graefe, *Vela erunt. Die Zeltdächer römischer Theater und ähnlicher Anlagen* (Mainz, 1979).
25 See note 23, Kraus, pl. 65.
26 Bieber, *History*, fig. 713ff.
27 See Pickard-Cambridge, *DFA*, 232ff. and T.B.L. Webster, *The Greek Chorus* (London, 1970).
28 For the definition of illustration see E. Zwierlein-Diehl, *Gnomon* 47, 1975, 65.
29 See L. Sécham, *Études sur la Tragédie Grecque* (Paris, 1926), Trendall/ Webster and A. Kossatz-Deissmann, *Dramen des Aischylos auf Westgriechischen Vasen* (1978).
30 M. Schmidt, *Antike Kunst*, 10, 1967, 70ff. There it is interpreted as a dithyrambic chorus; but against this see note 6, Froning, 23ff.
31 In special issue, *Schweizerische Kunst und Antiquitätenmesse* (1974).
32 For the arrangement of the tragic chorus see note 5.
33 See A. Greifenhagen, *Antike Kunstwerke* (Berlin, 1960), pl. 40f.
34 Carl Zuckmayer records in his Memoirs, *Als wärs ein Stück von mir*, (Fischer-Bücherei, 1969), 38f., an interesting episode with the actor Werner Krauss, who despised actors 'who had to perform through mimicry. These were mere grimacers. Poetic works were not written for this purpose. It should really be possible to depict the great figures of poetic drama with a mask. Therein lay the truth. He knew that in classical antiquity not only the gods, but even the great tragic figures such as Agamemnon and Oedipus were played with masks. He had secretly always wanted to do this.' Zuckmayer then related how Krauss took an Austrian peasant mask which happened to be in the house and played various scenes with it, and repeatedly changed its expression by the magic of his acting.
35 See L. Talcott, *Hesperia* 8, 1939, 267ff. and Pickard-Cambridge, *DFA*, 180f. fig. 32.
36 See B. Ashmole and N. Yalouris, *Olympia: The sculptures of the temple of Zeus* (London, 1967), fig. 113.
37 See H. Bulle, *Weihebild eines tragischen Dichters. Corolla Ludwig Curtius* (Stuttgart, 1937), 151ff. There is a new reconstruction of this fragment in the Martin von Wagner Museum, Würzburg, see note 6, Froning, 11f. pl. 1,1.
38 For their interpretation see E. Buschor in Furtwängler and Reichhold,

Griech. Vasenmalerei III (Munich, 1932) 134f., Webster, *GTP*, 41f. and see note 6, Froning, 8f.

39   See H. Bulle, *Von griechischen Schauspielern und Vasenmalern. Festschrift James Loeb* (Munich, 1930) 5ff. Pickard-Cambridge, *DFA*, 188f. fig. 54 a and b, Ghiron-Bistagne, 106 and coloured frontispiece and Blume, pl. 6. On the interpretation see E. Simon, *Tereus. Festschrift des Kronberg-Gymnasiums* (Aschaffenburg, 1968), 155ff.

40   See L. Curtius, *Die Wandmalerei Pompejis* (2nd edn, Hildescheim, 1960), 275 fig. 163, Pickard-Cambridge, *DFA*, 189 fig. 55. Webster, *GTP*, 44f. pl. 13 and Ghiron-Bistagne, 104 fig. 43.

41   See Pickard-Cambridge, *DFA*, 189f., 193ff.

42   On this problem see Bieber, *History*, 22ff., Pickard-Cambridge, *DFA*, 200ff. and Blume, 96ff.

43   On the Thracian dress of the Eleusinian priests see E. Simon, 'Neue Deutung zweier eleusinischer Denkmäler des 4 Jhs. v. Chr.', *Antike Kunst* 9, 1966, 89. On the different form of the boots, see note 48.

44   E. Christopulu-Mortoja. *Darstellungen des Dionysos in der schwarzfigurigen Vasenmalerei* (Diss. Freiburg, 1964) unfortunately gives no illustrated material. The only black figure representation of Dionysus with long sleeves known to me is on a late sixth-century amphora in Bonn, see Bieber, *History*, fig. 80 and Pickard-Cambridge, *DFA*. fig. 62, an exception which confirms the rule.

45   E. Robinson, *Museum of Fine Arts Boston. Catalogue of Greek, Etruscan, and Roman vases* (Boston and New York, 1893), 180f. Nr.495. The calyx *crater* is shown on pl. 6 of the 1972 edition. Mrs. P. Truitt kindly sends me this comment from the inventory: 'P. Corbett wonders if it's Corinthian red-figure'. But since the krater comes from Ruvo, to which Attic vases were exported, it appears to me worth considering as of Attic origin. The problem must here remain open.

46   For example the portrait of Themistocles in Ostia in G.M.A. Richter, *The Portraits of the Greeks I* (London, 1965), fig. 405ff.

47   A. Rumpf, 'Classical and post-classical Greek painting', *JHS*. 67, 1947, 13ff.

48   Cf. Benseler-Kaegi, *Griechisch-deutsches Wörterbuch* (new edn, Leipzig, 1962) s.v. κόϑοϱνος. Confusion in archaeological literature is due to the fact that such an expert as M. Bieber wanted to derive the actors' shoes from the costume of Dionysus, who, because of his relation to Thrace, occasionally wears Thracian boots. These are riding and hunting boots, which as a rule were worn with a short costume or one that was hitched up. They were so closely fitted to the feet, ankles and calves that the right and left shoes could not be swapped, as could the wider kothornoi, which developed from women's house shoes.

49   This is a bell krater, now in Ferrara but originally from Spina. See G. Riccioni, *Arte Antica e Moderna* 2, 1959, 37ff. and Blume, pl. 5.

50   For hetaera with pointed shoes and reveller with hetaera's shoes in a komos see Pickard-Cambridge, *DFA*, figs 65, 69.

51   Hdt. I, 155; for the width of the kothornoi cf. Hdt. 6, 125; on their

proverbial and abusive use (because of the possibility of wearing them on either foot) cf. Liddell and Scott, *A Greek-English Lexikon* s.v. κόϑοϱνος (no. 3).

52 In *Münzen und Medaillen Auktion Basel* (1980) no. 103.

53 Melchinger, 66f. finds this portrayal 'unacceptable' and thinks of the chorus as moving in 'a fine unconstrained manner', like the figures on the Parthenon frieze. But these neither wear the kothornoi nor sing choral songs.

54 The passage in question is the fourth chapter of the *Poetics* (Vahlen edn. reprinted Hildesheim, 1964) 1449a. For the discussion of the passage see note 4, Pickard-Cambridge, 89ff. See also H. Patzer, *Die Anfänge der griechischen Tragödie* (Wiesbaden, 1962), 82ff.

55 See note 54, Patzer, 52ff.

56 In F. Brommer, *Satyroi* (Würzburg, 1937) and E. Buschor, *Satyrtänze und frühes Drama* (Munich, 1943). Webster, *GTP*, 131ff. took the Corinthian padded dancers for 'men dressed up as satyrs'. Unlike Patzer, he did not separate the three different 'inventions' of Arion. But we know from the satyr play vases how men dressed up as satyrs appear. Cf. note 60 and pl. 9.

57 See note 10, Arias, Shefton and Hirmer, pl. 45.

58 T.B.L. Webster, *The Tragedies of Euripides* (London, 1967), 48ff.

59 This is how it was at any rate during the fifth century. Of the late archaic poet Pratinas of Phlius, who is said to have written the first satyr plays, it is attested in the Suda that, of his fifty plays, thirty-two were satyr plays, even though he is defined there as a 'tragic poet'. Even later there were writers known as σατυρογράφοι, e.g. Demetrios (Diogenes Laertius 5,85), who is probably portrayed on the Naples satyr play vase (pl. 9). On Pratinas see Pickard-Cambridge, *DFA*, 80 and Snell, *Tr. GFI* no. 4 (p. 79ff.).

60 *Satyrspiele. Bilder griechischen Vasen* (2nd edn, Berlin, 1959).

61 The Fujita Hydria at the moment is on loan in the Martin von Wagner Museum of the Würzburg University. E. Simon, *Das Satyzspiel Sphinx des Aéschylus* (Heidelberg, 1981).

62 See note 10, Arias, Shefton and Hirmer, 377ff. pl. 218 and Ghiron-Bistagne, 84ff. fig. 33.

63 On the original, or in the reproduction in Furtwängler and Reichhold (this is frequently illustrated, e.g. by Pickard-Cambridge, *DFA*, fig. 49) eleven satyr chorus men are to be discerned. As twelve is assumed to be the number of the satyr chorus, and as the Papposilenus is not a member of the chorus but one of the three actors, (see the following note), one may probably add the young boy with the lyre, who stands near Pronomos, to the satyr chorus. It is true that he has no mask, but this is also missing from the member of the chorus who stands on the left behind Demetrios, who likewise is given a lyre.

64 See Pickard-Cambridge, *DFA*, 236. The fact that Papposilenus belonged to the triad of actors, may well explain why he too wears the kothornoi — especially on Italianate vases. See note 60, Brommer, figs. 47, 48.

65 See also the important discussion of the satyr play in Horace's *Ars Poetica*,

200-50.

66 A particularly good colour reproduction of the masks of Papposilenus, Heracles and the heroine, is to be found in J. Charbonneaux, R. Martin and F. Villard, *L'Univers des Formes, Grèce Classique* (Paris, 1969), fig. 315. The oriental princess has a round, white face (Reichhold in his restored drawings did not get it absolutely right). One is reminded of the comparison of the beauty of a young girl with the full moon, which occurs both in Sappho and also in oriental folk-tales.

67 On the satyr play vase in Naples, see E. Simon, 'The "Omphale" of Demetrios', *Arch. Anz.*, 1971, 199ff.

68 For example, the painting in the house of Lucretius in Pompeii, see G. Lippold, 'Omphale', *Arch. Anz.*, 1955, 248ff. On this theme in late antique art, see G. Poensgen, 'Herkules und Omphale. Zu einem neu erworbenen Gemälde des Kurpfälzischen Museums', in *Bibliotheca docet. Festgabe Carl Wehmer* (Amsterdam, 1963) 303ff.

69 See note 6, Froning, 10.

70 Demetrius, περὶ ἑρμηνείας, 169.

71 In the Martin von Wagner Museum, Würzburg H. 5708. See also E. Simon, *Pantheon* 36, 1978, 199ff. fig. 1ff.

72 Snell, *Tr. GFI*, 120 n. 20.

73 The earliest drama known to us which demanded a moderately complicated backdrop and even a change of scene, is Aeschylus' *Oresteia*, which was performed in 458 BC.

74 See Melchinger, 82ff.

75 On this see note 13, W. Jobst, and the review of his work by H. Froning. *Gnomon* 45, 1973, 78ff.

76 See the definition by Pollux, *Onomastikon* 4, 124: 'Of the three doors in the skene, the middle one is either an entrance to a king's palace, a cave or a noble house, or it belongs to the protagonist of the drama.'

77 The valuable work on caves by W. Jobst is too much influenced in this respect by the views which H. Kenner expounded in her works on the theatre. On these see M. Bieber, *Gnomon* 28, 1956, 133.

78 A.D. Trendall, 'Three Apulian kraters in Berlin', *Jahrbuch der Berliner Museum* 12, 1970, 168ff. fig. 10; 12 a-c, Trendall/Webster III, 1, 27 and Melchinger, figs. 19, 20.

79 For the Prometheia see G. Grossmann, *Promethie und Orestie* (Heidelberg, 1970) and S. Melchinger, *Die Welt als Tragödie I* (Munich, 1979), 159ff.

80 K. Reinhardt, *Aischylos als Regisseur und Theologe* (Bern, 1949), 77f. See also note 16.

81 For this drama see T.B.L. Webster, *The Tragedies of Euripides* (London, 1967) 192ff. and Trendall/Webster, III, 3, 10-13.

82 See note 78, listed with bibliography by Trendall, 168f. n. 27. The Apulian pelike in the Martin von Wagner Museum in Würzburg, which he mentions, has been newly reconstructed.

83 K. Schauenburg, 'Die Bostoner Andromeda-Pelike und Sophokles', *Antike und Abenland*, 13, 1967, 1ff.

84 Vitruvius, *De Architectura* 7, 1, 11. Agatharchos must have then been

very young, since he later painted even for Alcibiades (Plut. *Alc.* 16). However I see no ground to doubt Vitruvius' words. Mathematical or technical ability, such as one must assume for Agatharchos' invention, is usually stronger in youth than in old age. Aeschylus had adopted from Sophocles the third actor in his later plays, so why not stage painting also? Sophocles, the most classical of the dramatists, must have been particularly 'progressive' as regards stage technique.

85 See H. Bulle, *Eine Skenographie*, 94. Berliner Winckelmannsprogramme 1934, Bieber, *History*, 69 fig. 266, Trendall and Webster, III, 3, 43, E. Simon and B. Otto, *AA*, 1973, 121ff. and Newiger, 458f.

86 Webster, *GTP*, 162 calls such doors 'practicable'. The German equivalent is found, for example, in the productions directed by Johann Nestroy. The setting for Act I of *Höllenangst* is described as follows (Inselausgabe 1970, Band 3, 197): 'In the background, which should not be too deep, a big palace-like house with projecting bays, pediments and a balcony is shown. Onto the balcony a practicable glass door opens. The window on the right of the balcony is practicable, and (opens onto) the gabled roof of the house adjacent to the back-drop. Under the balcony is a practicable house door. Practicable windows were certainly also used in Old Comedy.' One need only think of the Phlyax krater in the Vatican, see Bieber, *History*, 132 fig. 484. Also Nestroy's bay window is an old motif of comedy. Cf. pl. 11,2.

87 Euripides, fr. 601-16, Nauck. Sophocles: St. Radt, *TrGF* IV (Göttingen, 1977) fr. 534-6.

88 See Bieber, *History*, 66 fig. 253 and Blume, pl. 7,1.

89 Only one wing of both doors is opened. On the Würzburg stage set (pl. 10 and reconstructions fig. 3.4) both wings are indeed open but it appears here that the vase painter has taken perspective too far since a column is painted in front of one of the wings of the door and therefore this wing cannot have been movable on the flat back-drop.

90 Webster, *GTP*, 105 thinks the vase painter has duplicated the central door. To me this explanation is not convincing. When we work on the basis of Pollux (4, 124), only one of the two doors on the Würzburg (and Paris) stage set can be the middle door. The other is the right door. In my opinion the left door on both vase paintings is not represented, since, according to Pollux, it was not used in tragedy. The architectural sets which are attested on both vases thus stood not centrally on the stage but rather shifted to the right. This may seem surprising, but it appears to me that the strictly symmetrical reconstructions of classical stage sets (e.g. Bieber, *History*, 60 fig. 239ff.) must be revised. More on this problem in the publication of a new reconstruction of the Würzburg stage set, by B. Otto and the author, see note 85.

91 See note 18.

92 See Bieber, *History*, 124f. fig. 471ff. and Webster, *GTP*, 140 pl. 23.

93 Newiger, 483ff.

94 On the *Thyromata*: Bieber, *History*, 111f., 124.

95 Cf. the small marble reproduction of an early Imperial *scaenae frons* in the

Therme Museum. See Bieber, *History*, 182 fig. 634, W. Helbig, *Führer durch die öffentl. Sammlungen klass. Altertümer in Rom III* (Tübingen, 1969), nr. 2416.

96 See Menander, *Samia* in., C. Austin (ed.) *Menandri Aspis et Samia I* (Berlin, 1969), 38ff. N. Weill, 'La fête d'Adonis dans la Samienne de Ménandre', *Bull. Corr. Hell.*, 94, 1970, 591ff. Here there is mention of a feast of Adonis which had previously taken place. The *Zographos* of Diphilos probably had this festival as its actual setting (Fr. 43, 30ff. Kock).

97 See E.R. Curtius, *Europäische Literatur und lateinisches Mittelalter*, (Bern, 1965), 202ff. and G. Schönbeck, *Der 'Locus amoenus' von Homer bis Horaze* (Diss. Heidelberg, 1962).

98 Aeschylus, Fr. 128-133 Mette. Poseidon and Amymone in a (stylized) cave near a fountain house; also on an early Apulian pelike in Zürich, see *Bull. Ant. Beschau.* 46, 1971, 137, fig. 3.

99 See Pickard-Cambridge, *DFA*, 82f., Newiger, 479ff. Cf. also p. 14 and pl. 6,2.

100 See Bieber, *History*, figs. 133ff., 330ff. and T.B.L. Webster, 'Monuments illustrating Old and Middle Comedy', *Inst. Class. Stud. London, Bull.* Suppl. 23 (1969).

101 For an obvious male idol of this form see J. Mellaart, *Earliest Civilizations of the Near East* (London, 1965), 96 fig. 77. It shows the hunchback stance, which could also be adopted by the archaic 'padded dancers'.

102 On the 'Rural Dionysia', see Pickard-Cambridge, *DFA*, 42ff.

103 See Newiger, 492f.

104 See note 56.

105 See Webster, *GTP*, 29f. 135. The most important vase painting in this connection since Brommer shows the return of Hephaistos with 'padded dancers' also admits of another possible interpretation, see E. Simon, *Die Götter der Griechen* (München, 1969), 219f. Abb. 204.

106 See Bieber, *History*, 38 fig. 132. Cf. the following note.

107 See R. Hampe, 'Dickbauchtänzer und Diebe aus Korinthischem Krater', *JdI*, 90, 1975, 85ff. A similar view is held by Ghiron-Bistagne at 254ff. figs. 106, 107.

108 See Pickard-Cambridge, *DFA*, 246ff.

109 See H. Schnabel, *Der Kordax*, (München, 1910) and note 4, A. Pickard-Cambridge, 167ff. The latter writes 'Its exact nature is (perhaps fortunately) undiscoverable', but this appears to me to be too cautious. Cf. H. Herter, *Von dionysischen Tanz zum komischen Spiel* (Iserlohn, 1947). Herter also puts forward convincing arguments for rejecting the equation of satyrs with padded dancers.

110 For Demeter see Bieber, *History*, 48f. figs. 205ff. (the Kabiri vases). For Artemis see I. Jucker, 'Frauenfest in Korinth', *Antike Kunst* 6, 1963, 59f.

111 Cf. note 107.

112 See Bieber, *History*, 139 fig. 508; also there, many other examples of Phlyakes vases.

113 M. Gigante, *Rintone e il teatro in Magna Grecia* (Naples, 1971), 18ff.

114 A. Kossatz-Deissmann, 'Telephus travestitus', in *Tainia für Roland*

Notes

115 See *Bull. Inst. Class. Stud.* London, Suppl. 8 (1959) and 19 (1967). Further literature in note 113, Gigante.
116 See Bieber, *History*, 36f. figs. 123ff.
117 See S. Charitonidis, L. Kahil and R. Ginouvès, 'Les Mosaiques de la Maison du Ménandre à Mytilène', *Antike Kunst*, 6. Beiheft (1970).
118 Cf. K. Weitzmann, *Ancient Book Illumination* (Cambridge, Mass. 1959). For the illustrations by Dürer of Terence in Basle, see *Katalog der Dürer-Ausstellung* (Nürnberg, 1971), nr.152.
119 See Webster, *GTP*, pl. 21, and the discussion in the work referred to in note 17, 43f. pl. 5.
120 For the reconstruction by H. Bulle see Bieber, *History*, 124, fig. 470.
121 See note 117, Charitonidis et al., pl. 25,2. The eyes and mouth of the mask are not perforated, so it can be regarded as imperfect.
122 On the worry beads of the *hetairai* see K. Schefold, *Die Bildnisse der antiken Dichter, Redner, und Denker* (Basel, 1943), 162. The bronze relief illustrated there is also shown in H.G. Niemeyer, *Einführung in die Archäologie* (Darmstadt, 1968), pl. 7,2. The female figure on the bronze relief who is shown with the worry beads holds this attribute much more elegantly than Pythias on the Dioskurides mosaic. But these artists wanted to let one see in an amusing way that the *hetaira* is played by a man. Nowadays these worry beads are, in fact, a typical attribute of a man.
123 See note 117, Charitonidis et al., 46ff. pl. 6. Here too the earlier interpretation was on the right lines when it saw in the music players servants of Cybele and the text of the *Theophoroumene* confirms this.
124 See E. Lefèvre, *Das römische Drama* (Darmstadt, 1978).
125 See Bieber, *History*, 174ff. figs. 613ff.
126 See Bieber, *History*, 167ff.
127 See E. Nash, *Bildlexikon zur Topographie des antiken Rom II* (Tübingen, 1962) s.v. Theatrum Pompeii (Blume, pl. 12); the Marcellus theatre also, s.v. Theatrum Marcelli (Blume, pl. 13,1), and Bieber, *History*, 180ff., 184f.
128 See L. Friedlaender, *Darstellungen aus der Sittengeschichte Roms II* (9. Aufl. Leipzig, 1920) 124ff. On mime, see Friedlaender, 113ff. and note 124, Lefèvre, 449ff. and also in Lefèvre I. *Opelt*, 452ff.
129 See Bieber, *History*, 236 and fig. 783.
130 See G. Carettoni, *Boll. d'Arte*, 46, 1961, 189ff. Th. Kraus, 'Das römische Weltreich', *Propyläen-Kunstgeschichte*, 11, 1967, pl. 121. The masks are not 'satyr masks' as B. Andreae writes here. E. Künzl, *Bonner Jb.* 169, 1969, 374 fig. 31.
131 See E. Simon, *Die Portlandvase* (Mainz, 1957) 30ff. and *Jdl.* 93, 1978, 216ff.
132 See Bieber, *History*, 233 fig. 776.
133 See Bieber, *History*, 179f.
134 See note 128, Friedlaender, 119f.

Index

□□

Plates

1 Flute player and maenad from a tragic chorus. Red-figure vase painting, Athens, c. 470 BC, Berlin-Charlottenburg, Staatliche Museum, Antiquities section, Inv. 3223. Height 36 cm. Photo J. Tietz-Glagow.

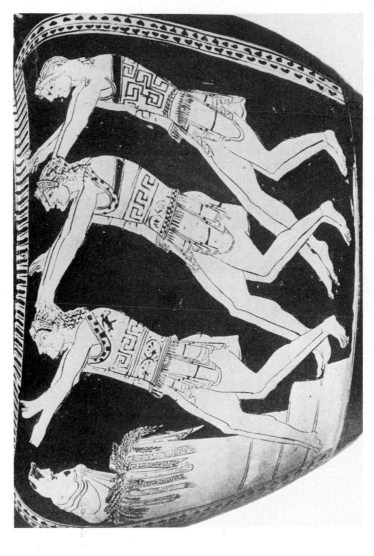

2 Tragic chorus invoking a ghost by its grave. Red-figure vase painting, Athens, c. 500-490 BC, Basle, Antikenmuseum, Inv. BS 415. Height 40.5 cm. Museum Photo.

3 Votive relief from Piraeus showing three actors, probably from Euripides' *Bacchae*, in the presence of Dionysus. Athens, late fifth century BC, Athens, National Museum, Svoronos No. 193. Height 55 cm, length 94 cm. Photo German Institute in Athens.

4.1 Mask of a young tragic heroine or chorus girl. Red-figure vase painting, Athens, c. 470-60 BC, Athens, Agora Museum, Inv. P 11810. Photo American Excavations in the Agora.

4.2 Mask of a young tragic chorus girl. Red-figure vase painting, Athens, c. 400 BC, Würzburg, Martin von Wagner Museum, Inv. H 4781. Photo K. Öhrlein.

4.3 Actor carrying mask of tragic king, probably that of Tereus, from Sophocles' tragedy of that name. Vase painting in several colours, Taranto, c. 340 BC, Würzburg, Martin von Wagner Museum, Inv. H 4600. Height of the fragment 18.5 cm. From an old photo.

5 Actor and mask of a royal character from tragedy. Painting from Herculaneum, buried in AD 79, copy of a Greek model c. 300 BC, Naples, National Museum. Height 36 cm. Photo Anderson 23415.

6.1 Actors rehearsing: a maenad and young Dionysus. Red-figure vase painting, Athens, c.460 BC, Ferrara, National Museum, from Tomb 173 of Valle Pega (Spina). Photo Museum, neg. no. 2139.

6.2 A comic chorus: men dressed in women's clothes and shoes. Red-figure cup by the Sabouroff painter, Athens, c.460 BC. Diameter 22.6 cm. Photo D. Widmer, Basle.

7.1 & 2   Chorus from Aeschylus' satyr play *The Sphinx*, which was performed
in 467 BC as the finale of his Theban tetralogy of which *The Seven Against
Thebes* survives. Five white-haired *silenoi* sit dressed in imposing draperies,
holding sceptres in front of the sphinx, who is gesticulating. Shoulder scene on
a red-figure hydria, painted in Athens soon after the play's performance.
   Private collection Takuhito Fujita, Tokyo. Photo D. Widmer, Basle.

8.1 & 2 Banqueting Dionysus and *silenos* as *kitharodes*; the satyr Mimus as flute player. From a fragmentary calyx *crater* by the Talos painter, Athens, *c.* 400 BC, Würzburg, Martin von Wagner Museum. Height of the fragment 17.7 cm. Photo K. Öhrlein.

9　Actors and chorus of a satyr play, perhaps Demetrios' *Omphale*. Main scene of the 'satyr play vase', Athens, c. 400 BC, Naples, National Museum, Inv. 3240. Height 75 cm. Photo Anderson 25925.

10 Backdrop (*skenographia*) for a tragedy. Vase painting with several colours (detail), Taranto, *c.* 350 BC, Würzburg, Martin von Wagner Museum, Inv. H 4696 and H 4701. Height of the fragment 22.5 cm. Photo K. Öhrlein.

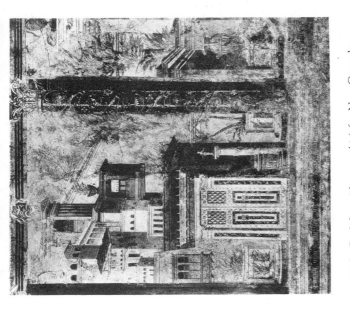

11.2 Backdrop (*skenographia*) for New Comedy.

11.1 Backdrop (*skenographia*) for a satyr play, possibly Aeschylus' *Amymone*. Wall painting, c. 50 BC, from a bedroom in the Boscoreale Villa, which was buried in AD 79, in the eruption of Vesuvius. After a Hellenistic model, New York, Metropolitan Museum of Art. From Ph. W. Lehmann, Roman wall paintings from Boscoreale in the Metropolitan Museum of Art (New York, 1953).

12.2 Mask of a *hetaira* from New Comedy. Terracotta, Taranto, third century BC, Würzburg, Martin von Wagner Museum, Inv. H 4683. Height 11.1 cm. Photo K. Öhrlein. Cf. cover illustration.

12.1 Mask of an old woman from New Comedy. Terracotta, Taranto, third century BC, Würzburg, Martin von Wagner Museum, Inv. H 4715. Height 8.2 cm. Photo K. Öhrlein.

13 Scene from the beginning of Menander's *Synaristosai*. Mosaic, signed by Dioscurides, from a Pompeian villa buried in AD 79, copy of a third century BC model, Naples, National Museum, Inv. 9987. Height 42 cm. From Hermann-Bruckmann, *Denkmäler der Malerei des Altertums*.

14 Phlyax farce. Vase painting of the Paestan painter Assteas, Paestum, c. 350 BC, Berlin-Charlottenburg, Staatliche Museum, Antiquities section F 3044. Height 39.5 cm. Photo Museum.

15 'Telephus travestitus'. Bell *crater* by the Schiller painter, Apulian, c. 370 BC, Würzburg, Martin von Wagner Museum, H 5697. Height 18.5 cm. Photo K. Öhrlein.

16 Tragic actor of the Roman
Imperial period. Ivory statuette
(cf. Bieber, *History*, fig. 799), Paris,
Petit Palais. Photo Museum.